THE MOST HUMAN RIGHT

THE MOST HUMAN RIGHT

Why Free Speech Is Everything

ERIC HEINZE

The MIT Press
Cambridge, Massachusetts
London, England

The MIT Press would like to thank the anonymous peer reviewers who provided comments on drafts of this book. The generous work of academic experts is essential for establishing the authority and quality of our publications. We acknowledge with gratitude the contributions of these otherwise uncredited readers.

This book was set in Adobe Garamond and Berthold Akzidenz Grotesk by Jen Jackowitz. Printed and bound in the United States of America.

Library of Congress Cataloging-in-Publication Data

Names: Heinze, Eric, author.
Title: The most human right : why free speech is everything / Eric Heinze.
Description: Cambridge, MA : The MIT Press, 2022. | Includes
    bibliographical references and index.
Identifiers: LCCN 2021010581 | ISBN 9780262046459 (hardcover)
Subjects: LCSH: Freedom of speech. | Civil rights. | Human rights.
Classification: LCC K3254 .H45 2022 | DDC 342.08/53—dc23
LC record available at https://lccn.loc.gov/2021010581

10   9   8   7   6   5   4   3   2   1

To Henry Steiner—without his initiation into human rights this book could not have been written.

The true goal of politics is not merely the least worst administration of the public good.

—PIERRE VIANSSON-PONTÉ[1]

Contents

1 INTRODUCTION

In 2005 Rakhmonberdi Ernazarov was imprisoned in Kyrgyzstan, accused of raping his former girlfriend's father. He was confined along with six other men to a cell measuring thirty square feet. Ernazarov was denied visits from his family and was seen by a lawyer only once. After a few weeks he was found dead from cuts to his body.

In the autopsy report, Ernazarov's death was recorded as a suicide, but his brother Mamatkarim had doubts. A prison guard told the family's lawyer that Ernazarov had been "subjected to constant insults" after cellmates heard about the charge of sexually assaulting another man. The guard claimed that Ernazarov "had been forced to eat and sleep near the toilet, that his dish and spoon had been damaged by his cellmates to make it difficult for him to eat, and that he had been forced to inflict injuries upon himself with metal cutlery." According to Mamatkarim, the prison guards had known about the abuse but failed to prevent it. The Boston-based organization Physicians for Human Rights later cast doubt on the verdict that Ernazarov had taken his own life.[1]

In another case, from 1998, an illiterate Iraqi, named "Q" to protect his identity, had fled Saddam Hussein's regime to seek humanitarian protection in Denmark. Danish authorities issued residency permits to him and his family. Medical examinations later confirmed that he had been tortured and suffered from ongoing physical and emotional trauma. In 2005, Q applied for Danish citizenship but was turned down for failing to complete his training in Danish culture and language. Under national guidelines, both physically and mentally disabled applicants could be excused from the language requirement, but those rules did not include individuals suffering from post-traumatic stress disorder. Denmark rejected Q's application, leaving him uncertain about where he and his family would live.[2]

Finally, consider the case of Alexander Kazulin, a former rector of the Belarusian State University and Deputy Minister of Education. In March 2005, Kazulin became chairman of the Belarusian Social Democratic Party. The following year he ran for president of Belarus, publicly condemning the dictatorship headed by Alexander Lukashenko since 1994. In the run-up to the March 2006 election, Kazulin was attending the national legislature as one of his party's representatives when unknown agents beat him, then tossed him into a police van. He was forced to sit between the seats with his legs against his head, choking on his own blood.

Later that month Kazulin took part in a national Freedom Day assembly in the capital Minsk, marching with others toward a jail in support of political prisoners being held there. Soldiers sought to disperse the crowd with batons, smoke bombs, and sound grenades. Kazulin was again beaten by officers and subsequently charged with hooliganism and public order offenses. After a flawed trial he was sentenced to five-and-a-half years in a penal colony, living in substandard conditions and denied basic medical care as well as contact with lawyers or with family and friends.[3]

These cases were all examined by the United Nations Human Rights Committee, one of several international bodies charged with monitoring how governments treat their citizens. The committee concluded that Kyrgyzstan, Denmark, and Belarus had violated the three men's human rights.[4]

CONFLICTS OLD AND NEW

In one sense, such conflicts are as old as humanity itself. From time immemorial governments have abused their powers. Ancient belief systems responded by holding rulers to high standards of justice. Over two thousand years ago, Confucius (ca. 551–479 BCE) sought to explain that government must follow principles of righteousness (*yi*, 義) and integrity (*xìn* (信). He encouraged officials to observe *rén* (or *jén*, 仁), by acting in benevolent and humane ways.[5] Just over a century later, Aristotle (384–322

BCE) warned that "passion perverts the minds of rulers, even when they are the best of men," while just law is "reason unaffected by desire."[6] In classical Islam, the concept of justice (عدل) requires that people within the community of believers be treated as equal before the law ("fair dealing").[7] In the thirteenth century St. Thomas Aquinas (1225–1274) wrote about why "human laws should be proportioned to the common good."[8] Teachings of Buddhism, Hinduism, Jainism, and Taoism embraced the concept of karma, whereby people could judge actions, including those of rulers, as fair or unfair, benign or harmful.[9]

Yet in another sense, Ernazarov, Q, and Kazulin's stories are very new. Traditionally the relationship between a government and its population had been viewed as a domestic matter.[10] Only in the twentieth century did experts come to view that relationship as a major concern of international law.[11] In the immediate aftermath of World War II, a handful of prominent diplomats gathered to explore whether they could identify human values shared by peoples around the world. Eleanor Roosevelt from the United States, Charles Malik from Lebanon, Peng Chun Chang from China, René Cassin from France, Hansa Jivraj Mehta from India, and others gathered to draft the Universal Declaration of Human Rights, adopted by the General Assembly in 1948.[12] I shall frequently mention that document, so you will find a copy in this book's appendix.

The Universal Declaration states essential principles in simple language. For example, according to Article 5: "No one shall be subjected to torture or to cruel, inhuman or degrading treatment or punishment." According to Article 7: "All are equal before the law and are entitled without any discrimination to equal protection of the law. All are entitled to equal protection against any discrimination in violation of this Declaration and against any incitement to such discrimination." To be sure, the more we contemplate even those two seemingly easy articles, the more complex they become. Does it count as slavery when people are so poor and wages so low that workers end up beholden to unscrupulous employers? Is it true that "All are equal before the law" if the wealthy can afford better legal services than the poor, or if men's courtroom testimony carries greater weight than women's?

For some people, those types of questions reveal deep flaws in the idea of human rights. Human rights, they argue, are framed in open-ended language, and can say whatever you want them to say.[13] Certainly, the rights listed in the Universal Declaration cover vast areas of human life. When stated so briefly, they inevitably depend on general language. The Universal Declaration speaks of the "inherent dignity" of all people, "the conscience of mankind," or "social progress and better standards of life," but do those concepts have any obvious meanings? Wouldn't different cultures view them very differently? Not long ago American courts were upholding slaveholders' rights to own slaves.[14] Today human rights law prohibits slavery.[15] Nothing in the concept of a "right" per se rendered one interpretation self-evident and the other unthinkable. Could it be that the malleability of rights, the possibility of interpreting their broad language in conflicting ways, precludes the possibility of human rights having any reliable meaning?

Not at all. The rights set forth in the Universal Declaration are no more or less pliable than the types of norms we would find in many justice systems. Justice systems throughout history have relied upon values conceived in general terms that can be interpreted in conflicting ways, such as "fairness," "reasonableness," "respect," "dignity," "honor," "decency," "utility," "prudence," "welfare," "necessity," "progress," "rationality," "public interest," "collective good," or "righteousness." Here are some easy examples. We read that one of Confucius's disciples asked "how to serve one's ruler." Confucius responded, "Do not deceive him, and only then will you be able to confront him directly [and deliver your admonishment]."[16] But what if the ruler is despotic, and would act cruelly on the information given? Or here's a famous one. Christian scripture teaches: "Do not resist an evildoer. But if anyone strikes you on the right cheek, turn the other also."[17] Yet hasn't acquiescence led to regimes that killed and brutalized millions?

The problem with human rights is not their vagueness. Like those older traditions, human rights have their own experts with their own interpretive toolboxes. If human rights fall because of their open-ended concepts, then pretty much every other justice system falls with them. The Universal Declaration's drafters knew that their brief document could not resolve all the complex disputes that might lie ahead. Instead, they saw it as a first step, "a common standard of achievement."[18] But then what went wrong with those older traditions—Confucianism, Christianity, Islam, and others? Indeed, after the European Enlightenment, all sorts of "isms" arose to promise better models of justice: liberalism, capitalism, utilitarianism, socialism, libertarianism. So what makes human rights different?

What *are* human rights?

In some countries, such as the United States, people don't always use the phrase "human rights," yet no people in history have been raised with a stronger sense of their rights. Some of America's most fraught conflicts have been waged on the battlefield of rights, including showdowns about racial equality, religious freedom, sex discrimination, the death penalty, abortion, gay marriage, police brutality, and gun control. Few Americans can recite the 1791 Bill of Rights[19] by heart, but popular consciousness often works more powerfully than checklists of rules.[20] In other countries too, people might not always use the phrase "human rights," yet the idea has crisscrossed the planet. In 1989 the world witnessed the Tiananmen Square protests in China, followed in Germany by the fall of the Berlin Wall, then in Romania by the Timişoara uprising. The end of South African apartheid, the Arab Uprisings, the global Occupy movement, Black Lives Matter, Hong Kong's Umbrella Movement, the global Me Too campaigns, along with street protests from Chile to Myanmar have all in some sense been human rights campaigns.

Virtually every important problem in today's world—poverty, racism, sexism, child abuse, environmental pollution, human trafficking, arms control, health care provision, corporate power, political repression—involves human rights. In 1990, with the Cold War at an end, Columbia University Professor Louis Henkin heralded human rights as "the idea of our time, the only political-moral idea that has received universal acceptance."[21] Was he right? Does our planet now live under a single, all-encompassing code of justice? Should it?

FREE SPEECH

In this book I shall argue that the contemporary international rights systems have failed. I shall make that argument by exploring the questions I have just posed, which many experts believe to have been settled long ago. I shall ask from scratch: What are human rights? I am certainly not the first to denounce the current international regimes. Some experts dismissed them long ago as corrupt and inefficient. Others see them as tools of Western domination: wealthy capitalist nations condemn others while dodging responsibility for their own abuses. Even those who support the current systems concede that they often do little good, suffering from chronic under-financing and scant cooperation from the most abusive states.[22]

Those arguments all raise vital concerns, but they will not be my immediate focus. In fact, I shall argue that those experts have never actually been talking about human rights at all. Decades after the signing of the Universal Declaration, we have witnessed countless rights documents and an intricate network of UN-based and other monitoring bodies, yet as a whole the international system cannot meaningfully be called a system of human rights. I am happy to call them systems of human well-being, or systems of human compassion, at least in their "on paper" aspirations. Better still, the current regimes can most accurately be called systems of human *management*.[23] That is how I shall describe them in this book. Their only task is to monitor the delivery of various *goods*, like shepherds tending their flocks, in ways that render any concept of *rights* wholly superfluous, or rather, wholly rhetorical.

The current international systems certainly cite documents like the Universal Declaration to identify human goods, such as fair trials or equal protection under the law. But I shall explain that there is a big difference between a system for states to manage human goods and a system for citizens to pursue human rights. Yes, Ernazarov, Kazulin, and Q did receive some succor (even if, for Ernazarov, it came only after his death), but not via anything that can properly be called an international human rights regime. Indeed, it should come as no surprise that the current international systems are rather indifferently viewed as accommodating Christianity or Confucianism, Buddhism or Islam, capitalism or socialism. After all, justice systems throughout history have taken on evils such as arbitrary killing, torture, inadequate food supplies, and other such problems. Yet if that is all our current concepts of human rights can do, then what can they do that other systems have failed to do? Certainly, there is much overlap between human rights and other models of justice, but my question will *not* be about what human rights do that other systems can also do. My question is: What can human rights concepts do that other justice systems have *never* done? If we cannot answer that question, then it becomes unclear why we should bother with human rights at all.

My question, then, is: What distinguishes human rights as a system of justice? I shall answer that the only thing that can turn government-managed human goods into citizen-directed human rights is free speech. In order for a human rights system to come into being, free speech cannot count as just another right on the Universal Declaration's checklist. Free speech within a safe and robust public sphere furnishes a necessary prior condition for the existence of human rights if human rights are to have any meaning distinct from the sheer management of human goods.

That idea, too—that free speech furnishes an essential foundation for human rights—is not new. Some experts will call it trivially obvious, others will call it patently false. One typical reply would be: "Of course we need free speech if we want to pursue our rights, but we also need food, water, health care, fair trials, and lots of other things. We can hardly fight for our rights if we are starving." Some would argue that all or most of the rights set forth in the Universal Declaration cannot be secure without all or most of the others, so no one right can be said to found all the others. They accept that free speech is as important as those other goods, but reject any suggestion that it is more important.[24] Yet my point will not be that free speech is more "important" than life, protections from torture, fair trials, availability of food and water, and other goods. If I live alone in the forest, food and water are far more important than free speech. My aim is not to rank human goods, but only to ask what is distinctive about human rights as a means of securing human goods—what turns human goods into human rights?

Many systems of justice—Christian and Confucian, Buddhist and Muslim, capitalist and socialist—acknowledge that people need food, water, minimally decent treatment, and other such essentials. Likewise, every ideal model of justice presupposes communication at some level:

basic norms of conduct must be communicated to members of society, and those in charge must somehow learn about people's needs and grievances. In that sense, all justice systems in some way involve communication. But I shall argue that the concept of a human right lacks any distinct meaning until it is grounded in free speech—which, moreover, requires democracy, indeed of a highly participatory type. Again, some will think none of those observations are new, yet the current international systems certainly do not reflect them, and do much to undermine them.

Free speech within the public sphere is the only thing that can render human rights different from other models of justice. As a result, there are very few states today that can even meaningfully be judged according to human rights criteria. Most nations are, at best, managerial regimes of goods and, sadly, that is the model our contemporary international human "rights" regimes have adopted. Imagine someone claiming: "Country X may not perform well on free speech, but has performed well in reducing torture and intrusions into private life, while increasing levels of health care and housing." It is the kind of claim one can hear daily in UN corridors. Yet it shows perfect ignorance about what a human right is, or what distinguishes citizen-directed human rights from managerial regimes of goods. Through millions of pages of speeches, official reports, and academic studies issued over decades, one could replace the phrase "human rights" with "human goods," and no change of meaning would result. That is why the phrase "human rights," as it is used internationally today, lacks all substance.

Yet it is far from obvious whether most people even want human rights, as opposed to simply enjoying some basic level of well-being.[25] Yes, protesters in recent years have often demanded human rights, but it is just as true that many of their fellow citizens never joined them. It is far from obvious that most people sympathize with the grievances of social groups to which they do not belong, even groups that have suffered grievous injustices. Some citizens, instead of commiserating, may feel annoyed by the claims of other groups. I shall not ask, then, whether human rights provide the best political model for all societies today or in the future. I shall ask only what must happen *if* we want human rights. To probe that question,

I shall first recall some historical background. Although I am arguing that the current international regimes do not steward human *rights* at all, I shall continue to use the phrase "human rights" in referring to them, simply because that is the phrase everyone has always used.[26] In chapters 5 and 6, I shall explain my alternative.

Some skeptics will still raise an eyebrow: "Look at the United States, the great bastion of free speech. Not only is it far from being a model democracy, but it commits one rights violation after another, both at home and abroad." For that and other reasons I shall have several occasions to discuss the United States, a country that pioneered contemporary ideas about individual rights, yet has often excelled more at preaching than practicing. Yet that objection would miss the point. My argument will be that free speech furnishes a *necessary* condition for human rights, not a *sufficient* condition. We certainly do not find respect for human rights wherever we find relatively free speech. But we do find the converse: in the very small number of countries that can be said to have genuine and strong human rights systems, we always find overwhelmingly safe and robust spheres of free speech thriving within strong democracies.[27] Admittedly, free speech today seems riddled with dangers. Licking their wounds after a Twitter brawl, some might feel that there is far too much free speech in the world. Can more of it suddenly guarantee human rights? False, dangerous, hateful, and provocative speech seems to jeopardize the very idea of an informed and empowered citizenry in pursuit of human rights, so I shall also examine questions about the limits of free speech.

This book must strike balances between different types of readers. For readers unfamiliar with human rights, one of its tasks is to sketch a backdrop (chapters 2 and 3), and to explain some basics about what the current regimes are and how they work (chapter 4). Those preliminaries are necessary because my own alternative (chapters 5 and 6), will make sense only with reference to what has preceded. For readers already familiar with human rights, some of that path will seem well trodden, but I hope will still offer a few insights. Meanwhile, in chapter 6, I shall review a few basics of free speech, which will be familiar to aficionados in that area, so I shall keep that discussion as concise as possible.

2 WHAT IS THE "HUMAN" OF HUMAN RIGHTS?

Human rights assume a particular conception of the human. Despite the trumpeting of a "Universal" Declaration, the UN document certainly does not reflect assumptions about human beings that have dominated throughout most of history. In earlier times, individuals' entitlements, duties, prerogatives or privileges depended on their social class, ethnicity, gender, or other status, which determined whom they would marry, to whom they owed obedience, and other essential elements of life. The individual human was largely defined by such bonds. Some ancient belief systems certainly preached abstract ideals of equality, but for the most part history boasts little evidence of pervasively egalitarian societies, particularly within larger civilizations, which often maintained strong class divisions.

In other words, human rights assume a notion of the "human" that has rarely existed throughout history. Human rights assume some essential sense in which all people are equal—in which the fact of being human is everyone's cardinal attribute. That point will become crucial later on in this book, since the freedom of speech that is necessary for a human rights system must include at least enough civic equality to ensure that all citizens can speak openly in the public sphere, be it live or online.

In this chapter, I shall tease out that historically recent assumption of *civic egalitarianism* by contrasting it with the historical norm of *civic differentialism*, whereby one's duties and freedoms are determined by one's social status.[1] I shall then correlate differentialism to managerialism—that is, to governments that provide goods and services without recognizing anything like individual human rights. By contrast, contemporary human rights presuppose some sufficient level of civic egalitarianism.

DIFFERENTIALISM AND EGALITARIANISM

"Slaves, obey your earthly masters with fear and trembling," we read in the Epistle to the Ephesians, written several decades after Christ's death.[2] To many readers today such words chime like justifications for oppression: "Wives, be subject to your husbands as you are to the Lord."[3] Throughout history we find belief systems grounding social hierarchies in the natural or divine order of the world.

Consider another ancient example. "Women and servants," according to Confucius, "are the most difficult to look after. They become insolent if you get too close to them. They complain if you keep your distance."[4] To today's reader, those words, too, sound like little more than a sexist and classist broadside. According to Yale historian Annping Chin, "This is the comment that got Confucius into serious trouble with women in the twentieth century. Many called him a misogynist."[5] Such passages adopt the standpoint of a target reader of Confucius's time, a patriarch, or male head of household, who plays husband to his wife, father to his children, and master to his servants.

Twentieth-century Chinese reformers criticized what some saw as "the ruthless Confucian suppression of women."[6] For example, a thousand years after Confucius, the master Ch'eng Yi (1033–1107 CE) would write in one classic text:

> **Question:** According to principle, it seems that one should not marry a widow. What do you think?
>
> **Answer:** Correct. Marriage is a match. If one takes someone who has lost her integrity to be his own match, it means he himself has lost his integrity.
>
> **Further Question:** In some cases the widows are all alone, poor, and with no one to depend on. May they remarry?
>
> **Answer:** This theory has come about only because people of later generations are afraid of starving to death. But [for a widow] to starve to death is a very small matter.[7]

Yet rarely can a justice system, ancient or contemporary, be called entirely differentialist or egalitarian. In any system we often find disagreements and changes over time. For example, the neo-Confucian scholar Chang Po-hsing (1651–1725 CE) later deleted Ch'eng Yi's comment. Insisting on widows' chastity seems to have been too extreme even for many conservatives.[8] People object to unequal treatment above all when it seems unjustified or arbitrary, and yet ideas about what counts as unjustified or arbitrary vary throughout history. Those Christian and Confucian texts nevertheless endorse differentialism by distinguishing between social actors according to gender and class. Male heads of households must follow one code of conduct, their wives must follow another, their servants another.

Interwoven with differentialism is what I shall call *hierarchical collectivism*. One's ethics depends on one's social status, and one's social status depends, in turn, on one's role within a hierarchical collectivity, such as a caste, class, clan, sect, kinship group, or community, to which one is deemed to owe ongoing duties. By contrast, egalitarianism correlates to *individualism*. The idea of the Universal Declaration that all humans share one ethics draws from its vision of humans as capable of autonomous choice and action. Certainly, families and communities continue to play a crucial role, and various experts have argued that human rights work to strengthen rather than to overthrow those interpersonal and social bonds.[9] Crucially, however, they do so in the sense of placing those relationships on a more equal footing, endowing the traditionally weaker members of those relationships with greater autonomy. Human rights presuppose both egalitarianism and individualism insofar as individuals must be able to assert their rights without obstructions imposed by governments, clerics, chieftains, fathers, or other traditional authority figures. The relationships between those concepts are illustrated in figure 2.1, where the solid lines denote concepts that, throughout much of history, have mutually implied each other, and the broken lines denote concepts that have mutually excluded each other.[10]

Ancient texts do not always explicitly cite, but do generally presuppose, a background legal order. Law in ancient societies was often local, customary, and unwritten, bound to a broader ethics, culture, and politics. Social relationships served to justify legally ordained hierarchies, which in

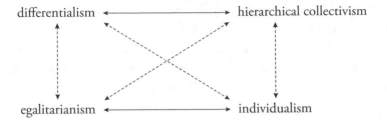

Figure 2.1
Differentialism and egalitarianism

turn entrenched those relationships.[11] Whether or in what sense notions of "rights" existed, for which many languages offer no easy translation, is a tricky question. In many societies heads of households exercised authority—and in that sense "rights"—over subordinates, but anything like individual rights held by underlings against the head of household, let alone against some higher authority, were at best limited, often nonexistent.

Even without mentioning law as such, Confucianism speaks with an eye toward rulers and officials. Consider another passage: "Duke Ching of Ch'I asked Confucius about government. Confucius replied, 'Let the ruler be a ruler, the subject be a subject, a father be a father, a son be a son.'"[12] Here too, one's legal and ethical duties depend on one's rank, echoed also in the admonition, "If you don't have a particular position, then don't meddle with any of its business."[13] Confucius certainly takes people's welfare into account, but mentions nothing about their "rights." Rather, such passages emphasize duties of a fluidly legal and ethical character.[14] Confucianism's conception of government is *managerial,* as it does not require anything resembling fundamental individual rights. Incidentally, the reason I am paying special attention to Confucianism is because it offers an early written corpus of advanced managerial thinking. We must take managerialism seriously, not only because the idea of human rights has been absent throughout most of history, but because, even today, it is by no means obvious that most people want human rights if they feel their needs can be met without them.

The foregoing Confucian passages, like teachings within other traditions, may at first appear to stress voluntary ethics above legal coercion.

Yet thousands of years ago, no less than today, ignoring "purely" ethical advice could turn out to have legal consequences, so the two spheres could not easily be separated. For example, a household, often larger than the nuclear units we know today, could face legal disputes if its domestic turbulence spilled over into provocations against members of a neighboring household, resulting in harm to persons or property. No fixed lines existed between the spheres of ethics and law, of private and public.[15]

We can now take a first peek at the distinct role that free speech must play for human rights. Many of the goods set forth in the Universal Declaration can in principle exist within pervasively differentialist societies, and could be provided without any concept of individual rights. Easy examples would be respect for life, refraining from torture and other inhumane treatment, or provision of food, clean water, or health care. Indeed, it would usually be in the ruler's and male head of household's interests to ensure that subordinate classes enjoy at least enough of such goods in order for them to be able to complete essential tasks. By extension, something like a guarantee of fair trials would also be logically compatible with a deeply differentialist society, even if in practice one would struggle to find historical examples of trials equally full and fair for members of both ruling and subordinated classes.[16] Other goods such as universal primary education and free exercise of religion would also be feasible in principle for highly differentialist societies, even if some persons in authority might worry about the political risks of the freedom of thought that those goods can stimulate.

And *that* hesitation leads us to one glaring exception. Aside from civic equality itself, only free speech for all within the public sphere has proven to be fundamentally incompatible with societies structured along overtly differentialist lines, given that respect for differences of class and rank traditionally means that individuals do not generally enjoy the freedom to openly criticize social superiors. In strongly differentialist societies, not only subordinates but even members of ruling classes generally lack full license to speak freely. When Louis XIV is feeling out of sorts, even the Duc D'Orléans measure his words. It is true that various empires and monarchies throughout history—Chinese, Persian, Roman, Bourbon, Japanese, Prussian, Hapsburg, Ottoman, and others—have at times known liberal periods, where expression was relatively free. However, as I shall argue later on, the level of free speech that human rights must presuppose does not exist where a government holds the discretion to grant free speech today only to withdraw it, and even to punish the speaker, tomorrow.[17]

And yet a puzzle still persists. Given that citizen access to public discourse presupposes a sufficient degree of civic equality, isn't it civic equality, and not free speech, that plays the foundational role for human rights? Of course, civic equality remains essential to human rights, and surely civic equality had to arise first as a historical matter, but only later will I be able to explain why it is not foundational in the way free speech is.[18]

AMBIGUITY AND ADAPTATION

Consider another Confucian passage: "Do not look at anything that is contrary to ritual propriety. Do not listen to anything that is contrary to ritual propriety. Do not speak in ways that are contrary to ritual propriety. Do not act in ways that are contrary to ritual propriety."[19] "Ritual propriety" (*li*, 禮) refers not only to conduct reserved for ceremonial occasions, but to models for everyday behavior.[20] Such advice certainly retains much of the spirit of the other passages. It, too, seems to speak the language of voluntary ethical duties, yet with tacit implications for law. It advises us, not least in our own self-interest, to refrain from deceitful, malicious, or contemptuous words and deeds.

Yet in another sense that passage differs from the previous ones. It makes no reference to social standing. Households or communities can suffer from hostile or adverse conduct by anyone, be they men or women, of higher or lower classes. The target readers may well be upper-class men, yet never does Confucius suggest that *anyone* is justified in acting wantonly. It would be wrong, then, to view Confucianist ethics as incorrigibly differentialist. Confucianism, like other traditions, turns out to contain intricate balances between differentialism and egalitarianism. For example, we also read: "In educating others, [one should] let go all preconceptions of class and [social] categories."[21] That comment heralds an important advance for a society in which it may often have appeared futile or dangerous to educate people from lower social classes. Some will respond that such contradictions between egalitarian and differentialist strands prove the incoherence of religion. Yet—leaving aside questions as to whether ethical and political thinking in a tradition like Confucianism can even be accurately described as "religious"—"secular" concepts have been equally subject to divergent schools and teachings. As we shall see in the next chapter, concepts of fundamental rights, too, have been interpreted in conflicting ways.

Those intricate balances confirm why ancient belief systems cannot easily be pinned down to orthodoxies. Different followers of such systems will strike the balances differently. That intricacy sheds light on how belief systems change over time, adapting to new challenges. At any given period we often find divergent interpretations of earlier norms and practices, and differences between formal norms and actual practices. Whether the differentialist or the egalitarian elements of a tradition are highlighted will often depend on broader political and social circumstances.

Moreover, as the twentieth-century philosopher Hans-Georg Gadamer observed, earlier interpretations do not necessarily equate with more authentic readings, nor later interpretations with less valid ones. Often it is not the immediate circumstances in which an ancient norm arose, but rather the passage of time that elicits persuasive interpretations. In Christianity, for example, the later emergence of Protestantism does not mean that it offers less convincing doctrines than Roman Catholicism.[22] Many Chinese today would expect greater class mobility and gender parity, and would not necessarily place the Confucian quest for social harmony at odds with greater civic egalitarianism. In that respect, they would render Confucianism more compatible with human rights than earlier interpretations would have admitted, allowing an ancient tradition to evolve just as other traditions have often evolved.[23]

Ancient Greece, too, reminds us of the complex relationships between differentialist and egalitarian justice systems. In his famous dialogue *Meno*, Plato (ca. 428—348 BCE) asks what virtue or human excellence (*aretē*, ἀρετή) is and how it can be acquired. Meno, who was born into an elite Thessalian family, is visiting Athens. He asks, "Can you tell me, Socrates, can virtue be taught? Or is it not teachable but the result of practice, or is it neither of these, but men possess it by nature or in some other way?"[24] Socrates offers no direct reply. He probes the question itself, arguing that we cannot know how virtue is acquired until we ask a prior question: What *is* virtue? Meno answers with a differentialist ethics as was common in antiquity:

> [A] man's virtue consists of being able to manage public affairs. [The woman] must manage the home well, preserve its possessions, and be submissive to her husband; the virtue of a child, whether male or female, is different again, and so is that of an elderly man, if you want that, or if you want that of a free man or a slave.[25]

That reply seems thorough but Socrates rejects it. Meno has recited examples of virtue, but has not defined it. Socrates proposes that they seek a definition together, but Meno quickly finds himself at a loss. Again, as with "justice" or "fairness," we often find ourselves in an impasse when we try to define an abstract idea like "virtue." But then Socrates has a hunch: "I have heard wise men *and women* talk about divine matters."[26] He seems to slip in an egalitarian wink, citing people revered for their ethical probity, irrespective of their gender.[27] He hints that we can acquire certain types of knowledge simply as human beings, irrespective of our identity or background.

And then he takes a further egalitarian step. Under a traditionally differentialist ethics, servants' tasks are deemed to be menial, not intellectual. But Socrates proceeds to interrogate one of Meno's slaves, who proves no less capable of performing a complex mental task than his master. Contrary to standard Greek differentialism, Socrates recognizes the slave as a rational agent, equal in that essential human sense to his master.[28] Also emblematic of Plato's egalitarianism is his call in the *Republic* for universal primary education, which was unknown in the ancient world, and would later strongly influence Enlightenment thinkers.[29]

In the context of Plato's writings as a whole, Meno's differentialism never ends up wholly refuted. Plato is no zealous egalitarian. In the *Republic*, he adopts a rigid class system of his own, although he presents it as derived from individual merit, and not, as in Meno's conception, on the inherited class divisions that prevailed in antiquity. Plato, like Confucius, presents a complicated picture. Neither can be stamped as altogether "differentialist" or "egalitarian." Instead we find each of them proposing a complex blend, partly reflecting their own times, partly seeking to make advances.

Despite his egalitarian steps, Plato's model society in the *Republic* is one that still differentiates among citizens in important respects. A coterie of gifted and meticulously tutored "Philosopher Rulers," bolstered by an exclusive class of "guardians," wields total power over the population. There are no elections. Once those roles have been determined, they remain fixed. One's ethics depend on the class to which one belongs. For example, the rulers adhere to a code that Plato deems appropriate for a governing class. They follow stringent norms governing their conduct, lifestyle, and access to property that do not apply to the rest of the population. Women may enter the guardian class and can become Philosopher Rulers, although Plato speculates that there would be fewer women than men.

In sum, Plato grasps the arbitrariness of Greek differentialism, and takes some egalitarian steps by seeking to correlate people's station in life to their abilities. However, his models of government in the *Republic* and his other writings by no means abolish class differences.[30] And Plato's *Republic*, too, is quintessentially managerial. The ruling class must tend to the welfare of all, but no one holds rights against the rulers. Of course, I made the same claim about Confucianism, which is not to call the two identical. They are worlds apart, which only confirms that humanity has invented countless forms of managerial rule and continues to do so today.

In Aristotle, too, we find both differentialist and egalitarian strands. Aristotle rejects Plato's division between governing and governed classes. In that sense, he takes a step toward a more egalitarian political and legal order, yet in other respects he rejects some of his teacher's innovations. In Aristotle's ideal society all citizens take part in government such that they "rule and are ruled in turn."[31] However, that citizen class includes only free males. Nature, for Aristotle, designs men to rule women and masters to rule slaves: "a slave is a living possession"[32] lacking any "deliberative faculty."[33] Women of the citizen class may well possess reason but they lack "authority."[34] Yet scholars today mostly read that differentialist element as reflecting the circumstances of late classical Athens. They believe Aristotle's politics and ethics still have much to teach us, but no leading specialist any longer thinks that only upper-class males are born with the ability to grasp those texts or to act as fully-fledged citizens.[35]

With those Christian, Confucian, and Greek precedents in mind, I must nevertheless underscore that I have presented those traditions from a human rights perspective, which draws bright lines between a differentialist "before" and an egalitarian "after," suggesting an admittedly simplified and linear world history. In fact, if one believes in human rights, that perspective derives more from hope than from history. To be sure, few government officials in the world today will stand before the UN and publicly denounce international norms against racism and sexism, even when their societies are rife with such biases.[36] Yet not only public officials but also broadcast and social media generate plenty of reactionary backlash. Nothing could be less certain than the suggestion that we are all marching toward an egalitarian future.

FORMALISM AND REALISM

In addition to intricate and shifting blends of differentialism and egalitarianism, justice systems throughout history have displayed both *formalism* and *realism*. "Formalism," as I shall use that term in this book, refers to *rules and principles adopted by duly empowered entities or persons as binding or authoritative*. Today that generally means in written form, but history also includes nonwritten versions, as when a political or religious leader gathers an official assembly and orally promulgates a rule or principle. However, since my topic is contemporary human rights, I shall focus on norms adopted in written form, particularly as set forth in the Universal Declaration of Human Rights.

By contrast, I shall use the term "realism" (or "legal realism") to refer to the meanings taken on by legal norms in practice, that is, in the context of how governments, courts, institutions, and populations actually follow, modify, create, or ignore legal norms or practices.[37] Many governments formally endorse the Universal Declaration, yet massively violate its norms in practice. To be sure, the terms "reality" and "realism" have many meanings. Some people use them to suggest that there is only one reality, or only one human reality, or only one way of perceiving, interpreting, or explaining human affairs. Others use them to mean something like "pragmatism," that is, focusing law or policy on what is materially achievable ("let's be realistic"). Still others use the terms to mean something like "accuracy," as with a realistic estimation of the number of persons attending an anti-government rally, in contrast to officially announced figures. A portrait may be called "realistic" when the sitter can easily be recognized. In this book, I shall not use "realism" (or "legal realism") in any of those senses. I shall use the concept only in contrast to "formalism."

Here too, the dynamics between formalism and realism can be intricate and can shift over time. Imagine that a sign stating "No vehicles" has been posted at the entrance to a city park. Ordinary visitors who read it will probably assume that they may not enter in cars, buses, or vans. But what about bicycles and scooters? On a strictly formal reading, the rule sounds absolute: bicycles and scooters are vehicles, and therefore banned. But imagine that after the sign has been posted, people continue to ride in on bicycles and scooters, and police and park wardens voice no objections. In that case, the rule starts to draw part of its meaning from everyday practice. "No vehicles" turns out to mean something like "No motor vehicles." To avoid confusion, local authorities could replace the sign with one that reads "No motor vehicles." Yet they may keep the present one, believing that it could come in handy if ever the park becomes too crowded and they need to start prohibiting bicycles and scooters as well.[38] Similarly, to say that a government's adherence to certain rights set forth in the Universal Declaration is "purely formal" is to suggest that, in practice, it commits abuses without regard to the Universal Declaration. The rights are respected only "on paper."

We see, then, that four factors form part of the backdrop to human rights: not only the axis of differentialism versus egalitarianism, but also the fact that both of those can manifest in formal as well as real ways, as illustrated in table 2.1. For example, box 1 displays *formal differentialism*, whereby a justice system expressly adopts differentialist norms, perhaps by officially assigning greater rights or privileges to men and fewer to women. If that regime is rigorously followed, then it will also manifest as real differentialism (box 2). No society will fit entirely into one box, since formalism and realism offer two different perspectives, illuminating different levels

Table 2.1 Basic types of differentialism and egalitarianism

	Differentialism	Egalitarianism
Formal	**1** **Formal differentialism** Differentialist norms are adopted in formal law, irrespective of whether they are followed in practice.	**3** **Formal egalitarianism** Egalitarian norms are adopted in formal law, irrespective of whether they are followed in practice.
Real	**2** **Real differentialism** Differentialist norms are followed in practice, irrespective of whether they are adopted in formal law.	**4** **Real egalitarianism** Egalitarian norms are followed in practice, irrespective of whether they are adopted in formal law.

at which law operates. Note, then, that box 2 can just as easily pair with box 3. For example, a given justice system may formally adopt egalitarian norms by officially assigning equal rights to women, while differentialism persists in the actual practices of government and society.

By the same token, those descriptive categories can change over time. For example, fifty years later, we may find that the formal law has remained unchanged in the first society, yet women are in practice asserting greater freedoms. In that case, while box 1 still describes the "on paper" law, we can also observe some measure of *real egalitarianism* (box 4), although perhaps still blended with a measure of real differentialism (box 2). So the boxes are not intended to pin a society to one fixed model, but rather to offer a vocabulary for explaining how formal and real norms can emerge and change over time.

Again, some systems adopt formally egalitarian norms of the type set forth in the Universal Declaration (box 3), but that are then disregarded in practice (box 2). Indeed, Western democracies often come under fire for adopting formally egalitarian principles in law while failing to follow them in practice. Box 4 expresses the highest ideal of international human rights, namely, that actual equality can be substantially achieved, usually via box 2 as a stepping-stone, although the precise level of equality required to ensure "real" equality remains hotly disputed, and often echoes conflicts about optimal economic models.[39]

I have thus far stressed civic equality as distinctive of human rights. However, once the distinction between formal and real protections is in place, it can be applied to any right, as illustrated in table 2.2. For example, as shown in box 1 of that table, a particular state may not formally recognize the right not to be tortured, but that fact alone indicates nothing about whether the government actually practices torture. Conversely, a state *may* formally recognize the right not to be tortured (box 3), but that fact alone, too, says nothing about whether the government actually practices torture.

From those two observations, the scenarios in boxes 2 and 4 follow as a matter of course. A state may actually practice torture, irrespective of whether it recognizes any formal norm prohibiting it (box 2). Or a state may renounce torture, irrespective of whether it recognizes any formal norm prohibiting it (box 4). The same analysis holds for any other right, such as the right to a fair trial, the right of access to food, and so forth. In today's world, the top-performing states[40] display a strong synthesis of formal and real protections (boxes 3 and 4). The most abusive states often proclaim formal protections, but violate any real protections (boxes 2 and 3). With those theoretical concepts in place, it is nevertheless worth noting that, in today's world, box 1 remains mostly hypothetical. Most states have adopted "on paper" protections, irrespective of whether they provide real protections.[41]

Table 2.2 Formal and real protection of rights

	Non-protection	Protection
	1	**3**
Formal	**Formal non-protection** A particular right (not to be tortured, to receive a fair trial, to have access to a minimum amount of food, etc.) is not formally recognized in law, irrespective of whether it is respected in practice.	**Formal protection** A particular right (not to be tortured, to receive a fair trial, to have access to a minimum amount of food, etc.) is formally recognized in law, irrespective of whether it is respected in practice.
	2	**4**
Real	**Real non-protection** A particular right (not to be tortured, to receive a fair trial, to have access to a minimum amount of food, etc.) is not respected in practice, irrespective of whether it is formally recognized in law.	**Real protection** A particular right (not to be tortured, to receive a fair trial, to have access to a minimum amount of food, etc.) is respected in practice, irrespective of whether it is formally recognized in law.

* * *

To sum up this chapter, contemporary human rights are unthinkable without a concept of the human defined by civic egalitarianism. Some ancient traditions may have adopted formal norms of equality, but in the everyday realities of preindustrial societies, class, rank, gender, or other such classifications determined individuals' duties and prerogatives. To be sure, "ancient" and "modern" encompass diverse and complex patterns. In some ancient societies, official or prevailing norms may have been formally differentialist, while everyday reality included grayer areas between persons belonging to different categories. In today's world, legal systems do overwhelmingly adopt egalitarian rules "on paper," but these are often violated in practice. Moreover, that distinction between formalism and realism applies to all human rights. Many states have adopted purely formal rights against, say, torture, arbitrary detentions, invasions of privacy, or free exercise of religion, but continue in practice to violate those norms.

3 THE INVENTION OF THE INDIVIDUAL

As far back as the de-colonization and anti-apartheid movements of the 1950s, activists have emphasized the egalitarianism of international human rights law,[1] yet they rarely dwell on its individualism, even though the two go together. In the popular imagination the two values are often viewed as opposites. "Equality" has a ring of emancipation and social justice, while "individualism" often connotes alienation, selfishness, and cold competitiveness. Individualism is commonly perceived as a Western value, contrary to the desire of most experts to show that human rights weave through many cultures. But, as I shall argue in this chapter, the concept of equality, as presented in the Universal Declaration, presupposes strong individualism.[2] The individualism of human rights does not mean that families, communities, religions, and other such collectivities simply vanish. We continue to live as part of such groups. It means only that individuals must enjoy ample opportunities to pursue their rights even as members of those groups, and to defy those groups when it is necessary to pursue such rights.

Documents adopted within international organizations often suggest that traditional cultures and communities align seamlessly with human rights.[3] Although social groups have long histories of restricting the freedoms of group members, experts often assume that those constraints merely need to be loosened in order for any given culture to embrace human rights. As they phrase it, groups must allow individuals to "opt out" from demands they do not wish to follow, as if that were a minor step. Yet the historical transformation from compulsory to voluntary social bonds has made more than a slight difference in history,[4] and has never occurred at all in many places.[5] Short of famines, wars, and other such catastrophes, it is difficult to imagine any transformation that has more deeply disrupted human societies.

To take one example, the international Convention concerning Indigenous and Tribal Peoples in Independent Countries (ITP)[6] sets out to strengthen traditional communities while respecting individual rights. It provides that indigenous peoples must be able to retain "some or all of their own social, economic, cultural and political institutions,"[7] but only insofar as members "enjoy" something that, in earlier times, rarely if ever formed part of those institutions—namely, "the full measure of human rights and fundamental freedoms without hindrance or discrimination." The text adds: "The provisions of the Convention shall be applied without discrimination to male and female members of these peoples."[8]

I by no means condemn that development, nor have all members of such groups rejected it. I wish only to note that it signifies more than a slight adjustment.[9] For example, members of Nordic Sami populations played important roles in promoting the ITP Convention in Norway, Sweden, and Finland. Since that time, LGBTQ+ activists have organized "Sami Pride" and similar events, after some years of hesitation due to conservatism within their communities.[10] In so doing, the activists certainly pursue their human rights, but only by redefining those traditional social, cultural, and political institutions in more individualist, voluntarist terms, to include free choices of sexual and life partners. But then again, in those Nordic countries citizens have for decades reaped benefits from their broader cultures of human rights. Whether all social groups throughout the world can be expected to adjust so willingly to human rights remains far from clear.[11]

The concept of "human ontology" refers to some conception of the character of human existence. It certainly includes the ways in which social groups mold identity and existence. However, human rights make sense only through an ontology that subordinates family, community, and culture to individual interests—again, not entirely, but to the extent that those entities must be barred from obstructing individuals' exercise of their rights. The individualist ontology of human rights wholly inverts understandings that, throughout history, had dominated the relationships between individuals and collectivities. In this chapter, I shall observe how, in European political thought, the idea of autonomous individuals as the foundational components of society—overthrowing kinship, clan, caste, servitude, and other such traditional bonds—drove the invention of human rights.

INDIVIDUALISM AND ABSOLUTISM

From the end of the Roman Empire in the fifth century to the Protestant Reformation in the early sixteenth, geographical borders scarcely existed in Europe. There were no maps of the world, like those with which many of us grew up, displaying one country in blue, another in green, another in orange. Kings, popes, dukes, cardinals, counts, bishops, barons, earls, lords, and other higher or lower aristocrats and clergy regularly jockeyed for power. Monarchs competed with those still-powerful aristocrats and clerics. Birth was destiny, as one's station in life depended largely on the class into which one was born. Much of the population was poor, illiterate, and consigned to manual work. Politically powerful women were rare, usually high born, and often only filling a vacuum left by the absence of a husband, father, or brother. Life was far from egalitarian.[12]

The Reformation, coupled with steady economic growth, spurred important changes. Monarchies began to consolidate their powers, often with bloodshed. The residual aristocracy and clergy lost political ground, steadily looking less like alternative powers limiting the crown, and more like administrators subservient to it. Increasingly powerful European monarchs began to accept the idea of fixed national borders and populations, heralding the emergence of modern states, also called nation states. That is the world in which the idea of human rights would emerge. Many people today associate human rights with democracy, as I, too, will be doing. However, the modern system of nation states emerged in the sixteenth and seventeenth centuries through a strengthening of monarchies that resulted from the elimination or coopting of rival powers.

Only after the Reformation did prototypes of our modern wall maps emerge, defined in Europe by fixed and mutually recognized borders, containing settled populations, and governed by some clear and ultimate power or "sovereign."[13] The seventeenth-century English philosopher Thomas Hobbes (1588–1679) counts among the prophets foretelling what steadily became our modern systems of centralized states. Born during the Anglo-Spanish war, just weeks before the Armada reached British shores, Hobbes memorably quipped, "My mother gave birth to twins: myself and fear."[14] Later witnessing the atrocities of the civil wars in England (ca. 1642–1651) and Thirty Years War (1618–1648) on the continent, Hobbes wrote his famous *Leviathan* in 1651 to advocate absolute monarchy as a safeguard against social fragmentation and civic unrest.

I shall now discuss Hobbes in some detail, but not only as a historical backdrop. I shall later argue that the current international human rights regimes are far more Hobbesian than is generally recognized, which raises doubts about whether they can be called *rights* regimes at all. But let's first review some highlights of Hobbes's thought. One painfree way of doing so is to contemplate *Leviathan*'s original frontispiece (see figure 3.1), which depicts a monarch dominant over all spheres of life—military and civil, secular and clerical, urban and rural. Notice how the monarch's body consists of an ocean of nameless, faceless, scarcely human figures.[15] They draw egalitarianism to dystopian perfection. All citizens are equal because all are equally anonymous, equally disposable. The state is no longer constituted by orders, classes, guilds, or ranks, but only by individuals, yet none of them are in any way distinctive. Centuries later, with industrialization and urbanization, writers would develop ideas about mass society to describe how human herds and swarms dissolve all of us into oblivion. Hobbes's *Leviathan* had already laid a blueprint for that world.

In order to justify absolute monarchy Hobbes starts by asking what life would be like without law or government, which he calls a state of nature.[16] That anarchic world lacks authority to limit anyone's freedom of action. Hobbes curiously describes that freedom in terms of individual rights: "every man has right to every thing."[17] If I see a grape hanging from a vine, I may pluck and eat it. No one owns the vine, since without law there is no system of property or ownership. If you see the grape before I do, then you have the same right to it. We may fight it out, and the strongest wins. You

Figure 3.1

Frontispiece to Hobbes's *Leviathan* (1651)

may kill me with impunity, since there are no police forces, courtrooms, or prisons. Perhaps my clan will retaliate against yours, then yours against mine, hence the "war of every one against every one,"[18] where "nothing can be unjust" since "there is no common power" to determine "right and wrong, justice and injustice."[19] Life is "solitary, poor, nasty, brutish, and short."[20] We have natural rights to everything, yet no government to protect anything.

We would loathe that world, Hobbes assures us. We would eagerly enter into a social contract, surrendering our natural rights in order to invest absolute power in one unifying sovereign who will keep the peace and guarantee law.[21] Hobbes rejects representative government, given what he sees as its potential to fragment, dragging a society into civil strife. His absolute ruler holds full powers over all citizens and organs of government, which, in turn, hold no power over the ruler. Absolutism, too, has both formal and real versions. In imperial Rome, Putin's Russia, and Xi Jinping's China, we find republics "on paper." In practice, however, those regimes concentrate total power in few hands. Hobbes's absolute sovereign may kill innocent subjects with impunity, may punish subjects who have committed no crimes, may play favorites, monopolize commerce, extend patronage, and control or abolish the press at will.

To be fair, Hobbes *urges* rulers to refrain from using power in such brutal, arbitrary, or corrupt ways. He *recommends* that they adopt magnanimous and enlightened rule, assisted by competent officials, not least as a matter of self-interest, to maintain popular support.[22] But his absolute sovereign by definition cannot be bound to those suggestions. The ruler remains free to violate rights; or rather, members of civil society no longer have any rights, other than those that the monarch may freely grant today then just as freely withdraw tomorrow. Hence Hobbes's ongoing importance: in today's world, citizens may well have formal, "on paper" rights, but when a government can violate them with impunity, then people have no real rights at all.

Hobbes is the first major philosopher to derive law and government from the individual, indeed from individuals who all start out holding rights.[23] Earlier thinkers like Confucius, Plato, and Aristotle certainly ponder individual well-being, but with no such starting point. Yet Hobbes's strategy, which takes two steps, certainly seems obtuse. He sees us as possessing full rights in step one, the state of nature, only for them to be swept away in step two, once civil society has been formed. If Hobbes had merely wanted to propose absolutism, he could have done so without going through the rigmarole of giving us rights that he then takes away. All that would be needed would be for the ruler to impose any and all commands at leisure, for which there were plenty of historical precedents. Instead, he makes individual rights utterly foundational, but then utterly dispensable. To what end?

Hobbes does not just want the ruler to be absolute. He wants that ruler to be, and to be seen to be *legitimate*—not merely imposed upon the people, but also desired and accepted by them, which they demonstrate by making the great sacrifice, abandoning their natural rights to the sovereign. Hobbes wants to show that we would consent to absolute rule. Still today, dictatorships maintain the trappings of parliaments and elections to create the veneer of popular consent, however ridiculous everyone may know them to be.[24] Christian thinkers before Hobbes, usually seeking to counsel rulers to avoid abuses of power, had certainly imagined human beings holding innate rights, but Hobbes turns that notion on its head. Under his schema, we all gladly throw away our right to *have* rights.

Later on, it would become customary to explain democracies as "social contracts," but, again, Hobbes writes the *Leviathan* opposed to any form of electoral, representative, or parliamentary government, let alone fully-fledged democracy. Hobbes's ideal government is managerial, perhaps the one salient element it shares with ancient models otherwise as different as those of Confucius and Plato. In particular, no ruler can govern all subjects individually, so Hobbes plans for networks of officials with powers to adopt and administer rules, and indeed to exercise their discretion in doing so, but always subject to the sovereign's ultimate power to intervene. And one other point: while quoting the Bible in page after page, Hobbes actually draws ethics back to a wholly individualist foundation. On his account, there is no objective way to reason about ethical values, which, he argues, arise solely from individual feelings and preferences.[25] If left to our own devices, we would dispute endlessly, and perhaps violently, about such matters. Questions of right and wrong in human affairs must remain in the hands of the sovereign, who imposes solutions through sheer power.

Hobbes has long sparked conflicting interpretations.[26] Indulgent readers believe that the turbulence of his century explains his choice for absolute authority. Heralding him as a founder of modern liberalism, they point to his anchoring of government in an at least postulated consent of citizens. They also note his appeal to the sovereign to exercise enlightened and benevolent rule, and to abstain from the brutal and arbitrary exercise of power.[27] The state protects individuals' free choices within a safe and orderly society, although Hobbes adds the sole condition that the sovereign may always intervene. That indulgent reading certainly adds up to a managerial regime for securing and distributing human goods, but does not endow citizens with anything resembling human rights.

Meanwhile, we must not forget other interpreters, for whom that "sole condition" renders Hobbes altogether *il*liberal, indeed a father of modern totalitarianism, who talks the talk of the people's consent, as modern dictators often do, while justifying a regime that would allow unbridled repression through brute force.[28] And consider another approach: among the sympathetic readers, the political scientist James Martel goes so far as to argue that Hobbes does the opposite of everything I have described. According to Martel, Hobbes's plan is to strategically provoke the reader to embrace not absolute sovereignty but radical democracy.[29] Notwithstanding these multiple readings, my present aim is not to compare or to scrutinize various interpretations of Hobbes. As with other historical thinkers, my aim is only to recall the prominent political traditions that they have come to represent, and to ask how those traditions have paved the way toward contemporary conceptions of human rights.

To anticipate some of the argument still to come in this book, imagine a seemingly benevolent but absolute Hobbesian dictator, who proclaims a willingness to adopt much of the Universal Declaration.[30] Can we say, as many international experts would argue, that several dictatorships today do in practice guarantee some rights? Contrary to those experts, I shall be answering with a peremptory "no." I shall certainly concede that many democracies, such as the United States, can be woefully poor human rights performers.[31] At the same time, I shall also concede that dictatorships can provide any number of tangible or intangible *goods* found in the Universal Declaration. But I shall argue that, by definition, dictatorships do not provide those goods as *rights*, no matter how lavishly they may provide them. Goods are things of value, like protections from torture or decent housing. Rights are claims *to* those goods, so rights presuppose the genuine ability to claim goods. That is where this book will be headed: If there is no genuine opportunity to openly claim a promised good, including through public criticism and protest, then, I shall argue, there is no serious sense in which a human rights regime exists at all. For much of today's world, international organizations do not oversee "weak," or "struggling," or "defective" human rights regimes. Rather, they do not oversee human *rights* regimes at all. For now, however, there is still more to say about the history of human rights, so those arguments will have to wait.

INDIVIDUALISM AND AUTONOMY

Another seventeenth-century philosopher, René Descartes (1596–1650), equally contributes to inventing the human of human rights. Descartes never proposes any systematic model of ethics, politics, law, or justice.[32] He gains fame as an epistemologist—a philosopher of knowledge—asking what we can know and how we can know it. Far from diluting his contribution to politics, that focus on the foundations of knowledge strengthens it.

Descartes sees individuals as capable of reasoning independently of social hierarchies such as the aristocracy and the Church.[33] He begins by turning inward, as any individual can do, in order to examine his existing knowledge. He resolves to doubt all that can be doubted, which includes the learning he had been taught by established authorities since childhood.[34] For Descartes, the very act of doubting means that his individual thought process itself cannot be doubted. We, too, can reason individually without depending upon superior authority.[35]

Once the individual mind is viewed as unbound to such authority, there is no limit to the ideas to which it may rightly claim access. In 1859

John Stuart Mill would pen his famous tract *On Liberty*, urging the greatest possible freedom of thought and exchange of ideas,[36] yet that imperative is already implied by Descartes's 1637 *Discourse on Method*, which can scarcely be construed in any other way once the individual mind is viewed as capable of independent reason and judgment, assuming, as Mill would later do, that broad access to information promotes those processes. Another crucial figure to name in this individualist tradition is Immanuel Kant, who, in the eighteenth century, starts with a Cartesian focus on "pure reason," from which he takes a giant step further, devoting several major works to deriving principles of morals, law, and politics from what he portrays as independent, individual thought processes.[37] Today, given the capacity for social media to whip up hostility and violence with little rationality in sight, many observers look skeptically upon the rationalist tradition, just as Hobbes had looked skeptically upon autonomous individual reason before Kant or Mill were born. But Cartesian rationalism, whereby individuals maintain the capacity to speak soundly about their own needs and aspirations, forms an essential part of the individualism of human rights.[38] Those who who reject it must accept government by managerial elites.

Despite their differences, Hobbes and Descartes present two sides of the same coin. Both adopt one ultimate authority that frees us from of all other social or political ties. Hobbes binds us politically to the sovereign state and, ultimately, to nothing else; Descartes binds us intellectually to our own reasoning capacities and, ultimately, to nothing else. For both men, some writers have seen those steps as an emancipation of the individual from the shackles of traditionalist forms of power and authority. People favorable to human rights are more likely to take that view. Others have read it as the wholesale destruction of precious bonds of religion, community, and family within hierarchical collectivities. Persons who take that view are more likely to be skeptical about human rights. The Hobbesian sovereign may order us to obey some high priest; but then it is the sovereign, not the priest, who commands and who can always reverse the command. Descartes uses reason to construct an omniscient and omnipotent God, yet, on Descartes's own terms, that same thought process must doubt God's existence if superior arguments should prove any step in that process to be flawed.

Certainly, figures in many times and cultures before Descartes have emphasized the importance of individual reason. Yet, just as Hobbes is the first to derive all of law and government from the individual, so is Descartes the first to base an entire worldview upon what the individual can independently judge. Some love it, some loathe it, but Cartesian individualism furnishes the quintessential ontology of human rights. As I mentioned in chapter 1, many ancient traditions today—Confucianism, Christianity, Islam, and others—may credibly claim to adapt to human rights, but they can do so only on the condition that the ontology of human rights is deeply individualist.[39]

THE ENLIGHTENMENT AND ITS AFTERMATH

Hobbes rejected fundamental individual rights as being at odds with absolute rule. Individuals sacrificed their natural rights in order to live safely within civil society. By contrast, toward the end of Hobbes's tempestuous century, his compatriot John Locke (1632–1704) endeavored to strengthen both natural rights *and* the social contract, each securing the other.

For Locke, the social contract exists not to overthrow the rights we enjoy in nature, but to safeguard them. Recall that Hobbes's absolutist "contract" scarcely ends up containing anything seriously bargained at all. By contrast, in his *Second Treatise of Government* (1689), Locke ushers in the Enlightenment by proposing a model of representative government that would allow opportunities for ongoing negotiation between citizens and public officials. Locke certainly had historical precedents, notably the Roman republic. Hobbes, like many others at the time viewed republicanism as factious and unstable, leaving a nation vulnerable to civil unrest as well as foreign invasions. Hobbes had described omnipotent government as the cure for injustice; Locke sees it is the cause. For Locke, government can only use its power legitimately when it respects citizens' rights to life, liberty, and property, which serve to prevent absolutism's oppressive potential. Those are natural rights that we never abandon.[40]

Far from discretionary, hence illusory, the protection of individual rights remains, for Locke, one of government's central tasks. Government can perform that task only when it is designed to prevent the rise of an overly powerful ruler. A century later, drafting the Declaration of Independence in 1776, Thomas Jefferson would assert Americans' "unalienable Rights." Jefferson adds that the purpose of government is "to secure these rights," and that governments "deriv[e] their just powers from the consent of the governed." Jefferson concludes that "whenever any Form of Government becomes destructive of these ends, it is the Right of the People to alter or to abolish it, and to institute new Government."[41] With each of those claims Jefferson is quoting from Locke's *Second Treatise* more or less verbatim.

In order to protect citizens' rights by limiting the ruling powers, government must be separated into legislative, executive, and judicial branches.[42] Those branches must check and balance each other so that no single branch of government gains too much power. When one branch becomes powerful enough to overwhelm the others, it also becomes powerful enough to oppress the citizenry. So Locke seeks to prevent all-powerful government in two ways. First, he structures government so that none of its branches can exercise too much power, and each places limits on the others. Second, citizens maintain their natural rights, so they, too, can legitimately act to limit government power and its abuse.

Yet there is also continuity from Hobbes to Locke. For Locke, too, the individual is construed *as* an individual, and not as an exponent of any ultimately authoritative community, religion, kinship group, or clan. Locke bridges the gap from earlier ideas about rights to modern ones. Again, rulers had long been, at best, *advised* and *encouraged* to respect their subjects' or citizens' interests, but Locke ushers in individual rights that can be secured by law. In so doing, he paves the way toward what we today call "higher-order" or "higher-law" rights. In the United States these are usually called "constitutional" rights, and internationally they are more commonly called "human rights." Other frequent terms are "fundamental rights" or "basic rights," and all these concepts are often used interchangeably.[43] Insofar as a common thread runs through those terms, one way to summarize their general idea would run as follows: *Higher-order rights exist where legal systems provide exceptional legal protections to certain individual interests, such that the people or the government, even by majority vote, either may not override those rights at all, or may override them only with some exceptional justification of its own, based on a strong public interest.*[44] Admittedly, terms such as "exceptional" and "strong" join our already long lists of ambiguous and open-ended terminologies of justice. Those types of qualifiers have long sparked disagreements. The Lockean constitutionalist tradition cannot resolve such questions in advance for each and every possible dispute. It offers only an orientation.

Locke, too, has sparked controversies. Admirers see him as handing citizens a genuine regime of rights, along with prospects of individual political empowerment. But skeptics have long condemned him for emphasizing private property rights, which furnished a legal foundation for capitalism, seen as entrenching class differences, empowering an elite only at the price of disempowering most ordinary people. For Karl Marx, Lockean individual rights merely recapitulate the interests of Europe's emerging merchant, or bourgeois class setting up for itself a system of economic and political privilege. On that reading, Locke merely replaces an old oppressive elite based on birthright with a new one based on legally protected wealth, despite his system's formally egalitarian vocabulary.[45] Locke's critics also point to his disparagement of non-Europeans, whom he saw as barbarians, incapable of maintaining any genuine economy or rule of law,[46] in so doing penning a justification for colonial atrocities—speaking the language of universal rights while in fact writing only for privileged, white, male Europeans.

Once again, my aim is not to choose any one interpretation, but only to summarize the traditions of classical liberalism and rights-based constitutionalism that Locke has long represented. Locke contributes mightily to the individualist ontology of human rights. On Locke's own terms, insofar as anyone—your priest, your clan leader, your employer, your President—stands between you and the exercise of your individual rights, to that same extent you have no rights at all.[47] To this day, the Hobbes-Locke standoff has not ended. Today, when citizens and their governments place a premium on citizen participation, they are more likely to opt for forms of constitutionalism and the rule of law.[48] By contrast, when citizens become suspicious of or indifferent toward constitutional self-government, they more readily accept autocratic rule.

With the 1789 *Déclaration des Droits de l'Homme et du Citoyen*, and then the 1791 U.S. Bill of Rights, the individualist ontology was well in place, and the stage set for formally egalitarian human rights charters as we understand them today: *Les hommes naissent et demeurent libres et égaux en droits* ("Men are born and remain free and equal in rights").[49] While human rights do, then, have antecedents dating back over centuries, a glance at those Enlightenment charters confirms them as the immediate predecessors to contemporary human rights through their individualist phrasing and comprehensive enumeration of essential individual interests. The Universal Declaration would add further rights, but never fundamentally changes the Enlightenment conception.

Yet as the eighteenth century drew to a close, any translation of Cartesian rationalism into politics was teetering on collapse, as France's anti-monarchical Revolution, led by authors of the 1789 *Déclaration*, descended into the Reign of Terror. The philosopher Georg Wilhelm Friedrich Hegel condemned the French Revolution along with what he saw as its simplistically individualist assumptions. Hegel challenges the Enlightenment belief that, through individual reason alone, a just new order can be constructed from scratch to justify the root-and-branch overthrow of the established norms and customs. Hegel revives earlier, pre-Cartesian views that individuals live not as automatons, but rather remain always bound to broader ties of culture, community, and nation. He resists the individualist ontology that presents individuals as shorn from their social contexts.

Hegel reasserts the view that human identities remain embedded within community, culture, and history. While conceding the arbitrariness of the established aristocratic and clerical authority, he condemns revolutionary democracy for swinging to an opposite, equally arbitrary extreme.[50] Also crucial to Hegel's position is his rejection of Kant's Cartesian project of basing comprehensive ethical and legal principles upon abstract reason, without reference to history or culture.[51] He largely accepts sociopolitical status based on merit rather than accidents of birth, but reformulates cultural and communal foundations for a society whose groups are organized collectively.[52] Hegel, too, has sparked a wealth of interpretations. Critics have counted him, along with figures like Plato and Hobbes, among the architects of later antidemocratic, indeed authoritarian, regimes.[53] Others suggest that, in a world where democracy seems largely gestural, Hegel goes some way toward explaining the logic of the modern, managerial and bureaucratic state apparatus.[54]

Like the Hobbes-Locke standoff, the Kant-Hegel clash has not yet ended. On the one hand, Kant embodies the Enlightenment ideal of rational, deliberative, representative government through stable institutions under the rule of law.[55] Fast-forwarding to our own time, his heirs today are likely to have entered the middle class, to have received liberal education, to celebrate cultural and political pluralism, to respect liberal democracy, and to welcome cosmopolitan ideals including human rights. In a small number of prosperous and top-performing democracies,[56] this strand now represents a large part of the population. In more turbulent and less stable democracies, or non-democracies in which such individuals have lived or studied abroad, they are more likely to form proportionally smaller elites, or to be viewed as such. Hegel sheds light on the many who have been left behind, alienated from that world. Within today's democracies, many at the bottom see their governments as opaque and untrustworthy, perhaps controlled by external or hidden powers. Some may seek an organic bond to a collectivity based on ethnicity, nationalism, religion, or some other source of unifying stories.

But back to the nineteenth century, a generation after Hegel, the young Karl Marx publishes *On the Jewish Question*, which would become one of the most influential critiques of the 1789 *Déclaration* and of human rights.[57] Marx ushers in what can be called "the critique of formalism," which continues to fuel doubts about rights today. That critique runs as follows. Formally, according to the *Déclaration*, human rights exist equally for all individuals, yet for Marx, the decisive element is not simply a set of norms on paper, but rather the fundamental economic conditions, and the legal order which keeps those conditions in place. As long as immediate social conditions remain organized along lines that entrench elite power and privilege, rights can never be achieved with the universality that their literal formulations promise.

For readers hostile to Marx, his rejection of the Enlightenment blueprints for liberalism, constitutionalism, and rights paves the way for the murderous socialist dictatorships of the twentieth century. For sympathetic readers, who refuse to blame those misappropriations on Marx, his critiques dispel the Enlightenment illusion of rights as unequivocal agents of liberation. He shows how rights can be appropriated to maintain a repressive legal order, a role that some critics believe they still play today.[58] These critiques of individual rights regimes have exerted influence far beyond Hegel's and Marx's respective views, often cutting across conventional divisions between conservatives and progressives.

For the controversial philosopher Martin Heidegger,[59] Cartesian individualism reflects abstracted, deracinated, dehistoricized, atomized, mechanized populations, a view echoed by modernist writers of the period, such as Louis-Ferdinand Céline, Alfred Döblin, T. S. Eliot, and Ezra Pound, alongside painters like Georg Grosz, Otto Dix, and Pablo Picasso, who often seemed to be depicting Western modernity as *in*human. Heidegger challenged notions of the "human" and "humanism," which he, too, viewed as hollow, ungrounded formalisms. For this declared enemy of modernity, such concepts serve not to ennoble us, but to reduce us all to empty, infinitely fungible abstractions, turning us into so many products on a shelf. For Heidegger, a world that needs abstracted ideals of the human can never achieve them, and has already condemned itself to inhumanity.[60]

To be clear, I am in full agreement with the voluntarist assumptions of human rights, and accept that individuals must maintain as much control as possible over their personal, familial, social, and political circumstances.[61] However, if we underestimate these critiques, we risk misjudging the resistance sometimes voiced against human rights, and against the individualism that they presuppose. When the Universal Declaration was first being discussed, some skeptics dismissed human rights as a Western idea with little to offer non-Western cultures. Again, many traditions throughout history had certainly shared concerns expressed in the Declaration, but it was argued that other cultures had not historically construed such concerns in the individualist terms of human rights. In 1947, hearing that the Declaration was being drafted, the American Anthropological Association

(AAA) proclaimed in its "Statement on Human Rights" that beliefs about "right and wrong, good and evil" vary from one culture to the next. Many social scientists doubted that a document printed on a few pages could sum up the values of every people on the planet.[62]

For example, consider another passage from the Universal Declaration. According to Article 6, "Everyone has the right to recognition everywhere as a person before the law." Yet, as we have seen, few if any preindustrial societies ever had any general notion of the human, whereby all members of a community share equal civil status. The notion of the human is supposed to denote essential characteristics shared by all of us despite our differences. But what are those characteristics? One might reply that all humans surely do share some things in common—all of us must eat, drink, and sleep. Yet those traits are by no means distinctly human, since we share them with other species.[63] We might add other attributes, such as dignity or a desire for justice, but those broad notions, insofar as they translate across cultures, can mean very different things. If we were to take into account every variation throughout history, then the notion of the human would have to denote everything that everyone, everywhere, has ever done. Yet the Universal Declaration by no means accepts everything that people have ever done. In fact, it condemns lots of things that people across history and cultures have done, at least if they plan to continue doing them. The Universal Declaration deems that much of what humans do contradicts its concept of the human.

"Standards and values are relative to the culture from which they derive," the AAA Statement concluded. Teachings "that grow out of the beliefs or moral codes of one culture must to that extent detract from the applicability of any Declaration of Human Rights to mankind as a whole."[64] The AAA Statement was taking a stand against Western political and cultural imperialism, but then other observers accused the AAA of pandering to the opposite evil, ethical relativism, by treating all beliefs as if they were of equal value, robbing us of any criteria of ethical judgment.[65] Hitler's Germany and Stalin's Russia had certainly promoted their own "standards and values." Nazi values included openly renouncing any concept of the human that would denote needs, ideals or aspirations shared equally by all.[66] Soviet authorities adopted rights of a sort,[67] but which were easily exploited as justifications for mass repression.

Even leaving aside those modern forms of mass repression, many experts reject the view that we renew Western imperialism when we challenge age-old customs of slavery, female genital mutilation, child marriage, honor killing, widow burning, and other traditional practices.[68] Moreover, today's globalized commerce implicates all of us in abuses committed or overlooked by foreign governments. Our purchases of food, clothing, oil, electronics, and other consumables render us complicit in discriminatory or exploitive labor practices, environmental pollution, and other harms borne disproportionately by those who wield little political or economic influence.

Despite those ethical and political controversies, by the 1970s human rights were gaining in international prestige. Social scientists were starting to deliver messages different from that of the AAA Statement. Today, many seek to marry earlier traditions with human rights.[69] The legal scholar Abdullahi Ahmed An-Na'im urges us to view the relationship between human rights and other belief systems not as a "permanent antagonism," not as a conflict between the West and the rest, but as a bond of "synergy and mutual influence."[70] An-Na'im concedes that "the most immediate antecedents and articulation of this concept of human rights have emerged from Western (European and American) experiences since the late 18th century,"[71] but adds an important caveat:

> The moral or philosophical foundation and political justification of the conception of human rights as defined by the [Universal Declaration] can be found in different religious and cultural traditions. However, since the traditional theology of the major religions of the world, including Christianity, is not readily consistent with this specific conception of human rights, reconciliation will require a reinterpretation of some of the precepts of those religions.[72]

An oft-repeated story has become part of the folklore of contemporary human rights, rehearsed in many historical accounts of the Universal Declaration. The French philosopher and UNESCO member Jacques Maritain wrote about the drafting meetings: "At one of the meetings of a Unesco National Commission where Human Rights were being discussed, someone expressed astonishment that certain champions of violently opposed ideologies had agreed on a list of those rights. 'Yes,' they said, 'we agree about the rights *but on condition that no one asks us why.*'"[73]

That anecdote is often recited as if it proves a home truth, that grit and pragmatism triumph over dogma and ideology. Yet few writers have noticed the next sentence, where Maritain concludes: "That 'why' is where the argument *begins*."[74] To be sure, despite the Universal Declaration's ambitious title, rights advocates today are content to focus on today's post-industrial and globalized world, without suggesting that fully-fledged human rights systems are universal in any sense that would have been appropriate throughout human history. Yet, as I shall be explaining, the only reason such agreement was so easy is because the drafters were not talking about citizen-directed human *rights* at all. They were merely talking about the managerial checklists of human goods that one can indeed find in many traditions.

RIGHTS SUBVERTED

Despite, or because of, the emancipatory language of the various Enlightenment-era charters, nineteenth-century governments failed to adopt many of those charters' provisions. Where higher-order rights were applied, it was often more to entrench a differentialist present than to pioneer an egalitarian future. The United States offers striking examples. In the 1857 case of *Dred Scott v. Sandford*, often dubbed the worst judicial decision in U.S. history, the Supreme Court certainly applied higher-law rights, but to uphold individuals' ownerhip of their slaves.[75] That decision recalls the malleability of the concept of rights. *Dred Scott* reminds us that nothing in the concept of a higher-order right inherently presupposes a socially progressive or even minimally fair outcome. Rights offer not iron-clad guarantees of justice, but a particular set of terms and tools for pursuing it.

Just over a decade later, in *Bradwell v. Illinois* (1873), the Supreme Court held that the Fourteenth Amendment to the Constitution, which requires states to guarantee to all citizens equal protection of the laws, was consistent with women's exclusion from professional legal practice.[76]

Toward the end of the century, in *Plessy v. Ferguson*, the Court interpreted the Constitutional requirement of equal protection under the law to be consistent with racial segregation in the delivery of goods and services, once again invoking a formal egalitarianism to justify differentialism in practice. *Plessy* confirmed the Jim Crow era of "separate but equal," promising formal equality but in practice leaving African Americans with few rights.[77]

By the late nineteenth century it had also become evident that many New York bakeries were operating in sites such as tenement cellars plagued by unsanitary conditions. Low-skilled workers with few options in the labor market landed in these bakeries, often compelled to enter into exploitative arrangements. In order to provide minimal protection the state legislature passed the New York Bakeshop Act of 1895, which limited working hours to ten hours per day and sixty per week. A few years later John Lochner, a bakery owner, was indicted by a state court for violating the law. The New York courts upheld the law, but ten years later the U.S. Supreme Court applied, though many have said "invented," a notion of higher-order rights of freedom of contract to strike it down.[78] Disregarding the economic pressures that forced workers to accept such dangerous conditions, the Court held that the Constitution protected the "right of contract between the employer and employees concerning the number of hours in which the latter may labor."[79]

Critics have condemned *Lochner v. New York* for adopting formally egalitarian rhetoric as if siding with the underdog employees against a state that wished to deprive them of their rights to bargain "freely" about their terms of employment. Writing for the Court majority, Justice Rufus Peckham saw the employees' interests not as imperiled by the owner's, but as identical with them: "The employee may desire to earn the extra money which would arise from his working more than the prescribed time, but this statute forbids the employer from permitting the employee to earn it."[80] Formally egalitarian reasoning is invoked to justify differentialist socioeconomic conditions. Any such constitutionally protected freedom of contract would further strengthen the superior bargaining position of the plant owner, who could then freely pick and choose contractual terms to his own economic advantage.

Given such cases, it becomes easy to see why Marx depicts human rights as formally egalitarian rhetoric deployed to maintain substantive inequalities. Again, that problem of abstract formalism is not peculiar to classical liberalism, capitalism, or human rights, since legal systems of various types must rely on generalities susceptible to conflicting and manipulated interpretations. That tempestuous history is by no means peculiar, then, to U.S. law. In all nations that espoused Enlightenment concepts of rights, prevailing social hierarchies remained inscribed in law. Britain, France and other European states were far from egalitarian in the nineteenth and early twentieth centuries, either at home or in their colonies.

Notwithstanding the injustices of *Dred Scott, Bradwell, Plessy, Lochner* and other such cases, it was by no means obvious whether the appropriate response was to work within rights regimes or to reject them altogether. In contrast to Marx, other progressive thinkers believed that rights offered the tools they needed. They decided that fighting for better interpretations of rights was better than fighting against the very concept of rights. In 1848 the women's rights activist Elizabeth Cady Stanton chiefly authored the Declaration of Sentiments, a manifesto presented to delegates at that year's Seneca Falls Women's Rights Convention. The document blends admiration for rights ideals with challenges to discriminatory interpretations of them.

From Stanton's standpoint, whatever ideas the eighteenth-century drafters might have had about what rights are and who ought to possess them, those charters would later take on a compelling meaning of their own. Gadamer again proves helpful: subsequent generations would read such charters under changed circumstances, drawing conclusions from their precise wording, including conclusions that some drafters might have shunned. Over time, the idea of natural, universal rights accruing only to white male landowners would become untenable. The Declaration of Sentiments tracks the 1776 Declaration of Independence in a way that may at first seem to mock, and yet ultimately honors that text. The Declaration of Independence had located tyranny embedded in monarchical power over subjects; Stanton reinterprets it as male power over women. The following excerpts, in which a few key phrases, sentences, and longer passages appear in bold type for emphasis (with some spacing inserted into the text of the Declaration of Independence), make Stanton's strategy clear.

1776 Declaration of Independence (excerpt)

When in the Course of human events, it becomes necessary for **one people** to dissolve the political bands which have connected them with another, and to assume among the powers of the earth, the separate and equal station to which the Laws of Nature and of Nature's God entitle them, a decent respect to the opinions of mankind requires that they should declare the causes which impel them to the separation.

We hold these truths to be self-evident, that **all men** are created equal, that they are endowed by their Creator with certain unalienable Rights, that among these are Life, Liberty and the pursuit of Happiness.—That to secure these rights, Governments are instituted among Men, deriving their just powers from the consent of the governed,—That whenever any Form of Government becomes destructive of these ends, it is **the Right of the People** to alter or to abolish it, and to institute new Government, laying its foundation on such principles and organizing its powers in such form, as to them shall seem most likely to effect their Safety and Happiness. Prudence, indeed, will dictate that Governments long established should not be changed for light and transient causes; and accordingly all experience hath shewn, that mankind are more disposed to suffer, while evils are sufferable, than to right themselves by abolishing the forms to which they are accustomed. But when a long train of abuses and usurpations, pursuing invariably the same Object evinces a design to reduce them under absolute Despotism, it is their right, it is their duty, to throw off such Government, and to provide new Guards for their future security.—Such has been the patient **sufferance of these Colonies**; and such is now the necessity which constrains them to alter their former Systems of Government.

The history of the present King of Great Britain is a history of repeated injuries and usurpations, all having in direct object the establishment of an absolute Tyranny over these States. To prove this, let Facts be submitted to a candid world.

He [the British monarch] has refused his Assent to Laws, the most wholesome and necessary for the public good.

1848 Declaration of Sentiments (excerpt)

When, in the course of human events, it becomes necessary for **one portion of the family of man** to assume among the people of the earth a position different from that which they have hitherto occupied, but one to which the laws of nature and of nature's God entitle them, a decent respect to the opinions of mankind requires that they should declare the causes that impel them to such a course.

We hold these truths to be self-evident; that **all men and women** are created equal; that they are endowed by their Creator with certain inalienable rights; that among these are life, liberty, and the pursuit of happiness; that to secure these rights governments are instituted, deriving their just powers from the consent of the governed. Whenever any form of Government becomes destructive of these ends, it is **the right of those who suffer from it** to refuse allegiance to it, and to insist upon the institution of a new government, laying its foundation on such principles, and organizing its powers in such form as to them shall seem most likely to effect their safety and happiness. Prudence, indeed, will dictate that governments long established should not be changed for light and transient causes; and accordingly, all experience hath shown that mankind are more disposed to suffer, while evils are sufferable, than to right themselves, by abolishing the forms to which they are accustomed. But when a long train of abuses and usurpations, pursuing invariably the same object, evinces a design to reduce them under absolute despotism, it is their duty to throw off such government, and to provide new guards for their future security. Such has been the patient **sufferance of the women under this government,** and such is now the necessity which constrains them to demand the equal station to which they are entitled.

The history of mankind is a history of repeated injuries and usurpations on the part of man toward woman, having in direct object the establishment of an absolute tyranny over her. To prove this, let facts be submitted to a candid world.

He [the male] has never permitted her to exercise her inalienable right to the elective franchise.

He has forbidden his Governors to pass Laws of immediate and pressing importance, unless suspended in their operation till his Assent should be obtained; and when so suspended, he has utterly neglected to attend to them.

He has refused to pass other Laws for the accommodation of large districts of people, unless those people would relinquish the right of Representation in the Legislature, a right inestimable to them and formidable to tyrants only.

He has called together legislative bodies at places unusual, uncomfortable, and distant from the depository of their public Records, for the sole purpose of fatiguing them into compliance with his measures.

He has dissolved Representative Houses repeatedly, for opposing with manly firmness his invasions on the rights of the people.

He has refused for a long time, after such dissolutions, to cause others to be elected; whereby the Legislative powers, incapable of Annihilation, have returned to the People at large for their exercise; the State remaining in the mean time exposed to all the dangers of invasion from without, and convulsions within.

He has endeavoured to prevent the population of these States; for that purpose obstructing the Laws for Naturalization of Foreigners; refusing to pass others to encourage their migrations hither, and raising the conditions of new Appropriations of Lands.

He has obstructed the Administration of Justice, by refusing his Assent to Laws for establishing Judiciary powers.

He has made Judges dependent on his Will alone, for the tenure of their offices, and the amount and payment of their salaries.

He has erected a multitude of New Offices, and sent hither swarms of Officers to harrass our people, and eat out their substance.

He has kept among us, in times of peace, Standing Armies without the Consent of our legislatures.

He has affected to render the Military independent of and superior to the Civil power.

He has combined with others to subject us to a jurisdiction foreign to our constitution, and unacknowledged by our laws; giving his Assent to their Acts of pretended Legislation:

He has compelled her to submit to laws, in the formation of which she had no voice.

He has withheld from her rights which are given to the most ignorant and degraded men—both natives and foreigners.

Having deprived her of this first right of a citizen, the elective franchise, thereby leaving her without representation in the halls of legislation, he has oppressed her on all sides.

He has made her, if married, in the eye of the law, civilly dead.

He has taken from her all right in property, even to the wages she earns.

He has made her, morally, an irresponsible being, as she can commit many crimes, with impunity, provided they be done in the presence of her husband. In the covenant of marriage, she is compelled to promise obedience to her husband, he becoming, to all intents and purposes, her master—the law giving him power to deprive her of her liberty, and to administer chastisement.

He has so framed the laws of divorce, as to what shall be the proper causes of divorce; in case of separation, to whom the guardianship of the children shall be given, as to be wholly regardless of the happiness of women—the law, in all cases, going upon the false supposition of the supremacy of man, and giving all power into his hands.

After depriving her of all rights as a married woman, if single and the owner of property, he has taxed her to support a government which recognizes her only when her property can be made profitable to it.

He has monopolized nearly all the profitable employments, and from those she is permitted to follow, she receives but a scanty remuneration.

He closes against her all the avenues to wealth and distinction, which he considers most honorable to himself. As a teacher of theology, medicine, or law, she is not known.

He has denied her the facilities for obtaining a thorough education—all colleges being closed against her.

He allows her in Church as well as State, but a subordinate position, claiming Apostolic authority for her exclusion from the ministry, and with some exceptions, from any public participation in the affairs of the Church.

For Quartering large bodies of armed troops among us:

For protecting them, by a mock Trial, from punishment for any Murders which they should commit on the Inhabitants of these States:

For cutting off our Trade with all parts of the world:

For imposing Taxes on us without our Consent:

For depriving us in many cases, of the benefits of Trial by Jury:

For transporting us beyond Seas to be tried for pretended offences

For abolishing the free System of English Laws in a neighbouring Province, establishing therein an Arbitrary government, and enlarging its Boundaries so as to render it at once an example and fit instrument for introducing the same absolute rule into these Colonies:

For taking away our Charters, abolishing our most valuable Laws, and altering fundamentally the Forms of our Governments:

For suspending our own Legislatures, and declaring themselves invested with power to legislate for us in all cases whatsoever.

He has abdicated Government here, by declaring us out of his Protection and waging War against us.

He has plundered our seas, ravaged our Coasts, burnt our towns, and destroyed the lives of our people.

He is at this time transporting large Armies of foreign Mercenaries to compleat the works of death, desolation and tyranny, already begun with circumstances of Cruelty & perfidy scarcely paralleled in the most barbarous ages, and totally unworthy the Head of a civilized nation.

He has constrained our fellow Citizens taken Captive on the high Seas to bear Arms against their Country, to become the executioners of their friends and Brethren, or to fall themselves by their Hands.

He has excited domestic insurrections amongst us, and has endeavoured to bring on the inhabitants of our frontiers, the merciless Indian Savages, whose known rule of warfare, is an undistinguished destruction of all ages, sexes and conditions.

He has created a false public sentiment, by giving to the world a different code of morals for men and women, by which moral delinquencies which exclude women from society, are not only tolerated but deemed of little account in man.

He has usurped the prerogative of Jehovah himself, claiming it as his right to assign for her a sphere of action, when that belongs to her conscience and her God.

He has endeavored, in every way that he could to destroy her confidence in her own powers, to lessen her self-respect, and to make her willing to lead a dependent and abject life.

Now, in view of this entire disfranchisement of one-half the people of this country, their social and religious degradation,—in view of the unjust laws above mentioned, and because women do feel themselves aggrieved, oppressed, and fraudulently deprived of their most sacred rights, we insist that they have immediate admission to all the rights and privileges which belong to them as citizens of these United States.

In entering upon the great work before us, we anticipate no small amount of misconception, misrepresentation, and ridicule; but we shall use every instrumentality within our power to effect our object. We shall employ agents, circulate tracts, petition the State and national Legislatures, and endeavor to enlist the pulpit and the press in our behalf. We hope this Convention will be followed by a series of Conventions, embracing every part of the country.

Another of Karl Marx's objections to rights was their fragmentary character—rights for minorities, rights for women, rights for colonized peoples. In his view, oppression did not take different forms, but arose from the common cause of economic exploitation. Hand in hand with that concern he called for unity among activists. A cohesive movement would muster greater power than competing factions. Marx's view carries some weight, given that the erstwhile friends Stanton and the abolitionist Frederick Douglass sadly divided over whether it was women or slaves who ought to take tactical priority.[81] Indeed, nineteenth-century feminists have increasingly been chastised for excluding black women from their movement.[82] Yet these activists did still share a commitment to building upon existing concepts of rights.

Similar to Stanton, Douglass exposes the incongruity of formally egalitarian rights applied to justify discriminatory practices in a speech entitled "What to the Slave is the Fourth of July?" Unlike Marx, Douglass does not condemn rights for their inability to do justice to African Americans. Rather, Douglass accuses the government of failing to do justice to rights. He rejects the rights culture of his time in order to advocate a more credible one.[83] Susan B. Anthony also pursued that strategy of reinterpreting rather than rejecting rights. She reminded a Boston audience that it is "we, the people" who author the U.S. Constitution—and thereby the entirety of the Bill of Rights—"not we, the white male citizens; nor yet we, the male citizens; but we, the whole people, who formed the Union."[84] Yet in their own time, Stanton, Douglass, and Anthony remained outliers, widely seen as extremist and indeed dangerous.

In the nineteenth century, then, we witness what would remain one of the intractable schisms in progressive politics. To this day, plenty of leftists insist on working within the system, following people like Stanton, Douglass, and Anthony. Yet there are certainly radicals who argue that the prevailing system only ever reproduces and perpetuates itself, and remains incapable of achieving comprehensive change, which they believe can come about only through a comprehensive dismantling of existing politics.[85] Clearly, human rights activists can commit only to the former option. Radicals are certainly free to reject human rights on that very basis—again I am asking only what is required *if* we want human rights. But radicals must then recognize that many such leftist rejections of constitutional democracy have, in the past, led at best to purely managerial regimes of goods, with little serious citizen empowerment over time, and at worst to mass atrocities.[86] Some might find it strange that I seem to allow only two models: managerial human goods *or* citizen-directed human rights, as if no other options were possible. But recall that I am not seeking the best possible politics, of which there are indeed many models. I am asking only about the character of human rights.

* * *

I have argued in this chapter that civic equality necessarily entails individualism, yet often with ambiguous historical and cultural significance. Thomas Hobbes was the first to derive a comprehensive political philosophy by starting with individuals who are all equal in their status as human beings—individuals subject to no binding ties of church, community, or kinship—but only in the sense that they risk becoming insignificant. Later writers, notably Descartes, endow the individual with a richer autonomy than Hobbes had done. Yet we can only think seriously about human rights when we acknowledge the depth of cultural change wrought by Cartesian individualism. Moreover, as some historic U.S. legal cases have reminded us, the concept of a human right, like the egalitarianism and individualism that it presupposes, by no means guarantees an emancipatory or progressive politics. What counts as emancipatory or progressive is often less obvious or agreed than we may think, but that need not deter the attempt to develop a better conception of human rights.

4 GOING GLOBAL

Cases like *Dred Scott, Bradwell, Plessy*, and *Lochner* confirmed long ago that the sheer existence of a higher-law right guarantees neither obvious nor ethical outcomes. By the early twentieth century the legal scholar Wesley Hohfeld (1879–1918) was lamenting that "the term 'rights' tends to be used indiscriminately" to denote all manner of legal, moral, and political interests. He quoted a Tennessee judge grumbling in the otherwise obscure case of *Lonas v. State* that "the words *rights, privileges* and *immunities*, are abusively used, as if they were synonymous."[1] I'll return to that case in a moment.

With Hohfeld we retreat from the grand pronouncements of classical philosophers and the cries of activists into the sleepy corridors of the law library. Hohfeld graduated from Harvard Law School in 1904. In a brief career he taught at Stanford until 1913 then moved to Yale, and died in 1918 at the age of thirty-nine.[2] For Hohfeld, popular moral or political concepts of "right" seemed vague and controversial, so he wanted to discover the meaning of a right "in the strictest sense," that is, in its distinctly legal sense.[3] A claim such as "I have the right to be treated fairly" may certainly carry moral and political weight, but what would be required for it to correlate to a specifically legal right? In this chapter I shall trace the consolidation of that legal concept of rights in the twentieth century, and the complex ways in which international organizations have responded.

Hohfeld never published any opinions concerning the blazing controversies of his day, nor do we know about his political leanings. His writings focus largely on ordinary rights in contract, property, and the like. I do find it hard to believe that a century of culture wars so bitterly waged on the battlefield of rights would have left no imprint upon, of all people, one of the twentieth century's pioneering rights theorists. Hohfeld may have believed that there was no point to tackling explosive controversies like discrimination before figuring out what we mean by "rights" in more workaday settings. Yet when we dig deeper, we discover, for example, that *Lonas v. State* was no humdrum dispute. Decided just a few years after the Civil War, the court upheld a ban on interracial marriages, as other American states had long been doing.

Meanwhile, across the Atlantic, amid the equally tempestuous twilight of the Austro-Hungarian empire, tensions were simmering between various countries and their national, ethnic, and religious minority groups.[4] There we find another titan of the legal world, the jurist Hans Kelsen similarly poring over the mechanics of legal systems, toiling to distill their essential elements. Born in Prague in 1881, Kelsen grew up just a few blocks from Franz Kafka, who was born two years later. I know of no evidence that they ever met, although Kafka would later spend his hours mercilessly spoofing the types of modern legal labyrinths of which Kelsen became a preeminent expositor. Kelsen authored much of the 1920 Austrian constitution, a good deal of which remains in force today. In 1930 he moved to Cologne, but had to flee three years after the Nazis came to power because of his Jewish heritage. He later settled in California, teaching at Berkeley until his death in 1973, aged ninety-one.[5]

After the European Enlightenment, many jurists had come to view morals, politics, and religion as irrational, subjective, and partisan. A movement known as "legal positivism" emerged, presenting law as a system operating according to its own internal logic.[6] Kelsen and Hohfeld knew perfectly well that laws concerning murder, theft, and marriage, for example, had first arisen within broader ethical, political, or religious systems, but they shared the quest to discover what turns a social norm into a legal norm.

A specifically legal concept of rights can be useful only insofar as law does things that ethics, politics, and religion do not do. None of their writings from that era suggest they were familiar with each other's work, yet over time their core insights on the legal character of a right would coincide. Both of them explain that *one party's legal right correlates to another party's legal duty.*[7] In other words, *X holds a legal right against Y only if Y owes some legal duty to X.* Throughout the rest of this book I shall call this the *duty principle.* Take an example. If Ringo has the legal right to cross Abbey Road at its intersection with Grove End Road, then other persons have a legal duty not to block Ringo's passage across it.

That relationship between rights and duties may at first seem obvious, but one trap must be avoided. Notions of duty are arguably as old as the idea of justice itself, found in many ancient systems. Would it be correct, then, to say that ancient systems had included corresponding rights all along? For example, assuming we can find norms in Confucianism, Christianity, or other traditions that place a duty on rulers to refrain from inflicting wanton violence on ordinary people, does that mean that those traditions included individual *rights* for ordinary people not to be subjected to such violence? Not at all. That is because the relationship between rights and duties is not strictly mutual. *All rights correlate to duties, but not all duties correlate to rights.* (In other words, it is true to say that X holds a legal right against Y *only* if Y owes some legal duty to X. However, it is false to say that Y owes some legal duty to X *only* if X holds a legal right against Y.)

Here's a simple example. Assume that a city ordinance grants me a legal right to have shrubbery planted by local government on a roadside near my home. In that case, the city has a legal duty to plant the shrubbery. If it fails to do so, then I can sue the city for redress. But now assume that the law mandates *only* that the city must plant shrubbery on the roadside near my home. In other words, the law does still place a duty on the city to plant the shrubs, but does not expressly grant me or any other citizen a right for the shrubbery to be planted. Now if the city government fails to plant the shrubs, I may write a letter to my local newspaper, organize a roadside beautification movement, or vote against the local government at the next elections, but I have no standing to sue the city. The sheer fact that the city has a duty to plant the shrubs does not automatically bestow on me any right to have the shrubs planted, unless the law additionally creates such right. (Incidentally, assuming the first scenario, where the law *does* grant me the right to have the shrubbery planted, it is worth noting that the city has granted me only an ordinary right, not a higher-order right—that is, not a human right touching an essential human interest, at least under a reasonably restrained notion of human rights. Ordinary rights arise in various areas of law, such as contract law, commercial law, and other branches.)

Many traditions throughout history have prescribed duties for rulers to act in particular ways, which may at times reflect values set forth in the Universal Declaration of Human Rights, but that does not mean that those traditions ever implied individual *rights* to have government provide those goods. That observation does not necessarily mean that any given tradition is incompatible with human rights, but it again reminds us that human rights law imposes great demands on any belief system that would claim to be compliant with it. Those who would hold the Universal Declaration in the right hand, and some ancient text in the left, may well find overlaps, but only of human goods, and rarely, if ever, of human rights.[8]

To appreciate that point, imagine a dictatorship called Regalia, which has issued an official document pledging to respect the Universal Declaration. Regalia delivers many of the goods set forth in the declaration, but only at the discretion of Bruder, its Hobbesian dictator, who in practice recognizes no such duties on Regalia to provide those goods. As I shall explain later in this chapter, Regalia *is* bound to recognize and to obey many of those duties from the standpoint of international law. By contrast, from the standpoint of its own domestic law, Regalia may well function as a managerial regime, choosing to provide or not to provide such goods at the government's discretion. On its own interpretation, when it does provide those goods, it does not do so as a matter of individual *right*.

We can say, then, that duty lies midway between discretion and enforcement. Under the duty principle, a duty upon the state to provide goods brings us closer to rights than the state's sheer discretion to provide them. Duties provide reasons *for* enforcement, even if they are not always enforced. Our search for human rights therefore involves a search for something more, something that can move us from a discretionary regime toward that midpoint, toward that point at which a human good, such as privacy or fair trials, first becomes the object of a human *right* to privacy or to fair trials. The duty principle furnishes part of the answer, but in the next chapter I explain why the additional ingredient is free speech.

Note also a further qualification to the duty principle: the fact that one person holds a right correlative to another's duty does not make that right absolute; and if a right is not absolute, then by definition the duty cannot be absolute. For example, if Mick crashes his car into a nearby milk delivery van on Abbey Road, then the police may have to bar pedestrians from crossing, including Ringo, perhaps by cordoning off the road. That kind of everyday contingency shows how nonabsolute many rights are, and human rights include such instances. For example, I may have a human right to privacy in my home, but that does not allow me to use my home for money laundering or selling prohibited drugs. Similarly, my human right to practice a particular religion does not authorize me to practice ritual homicide, since human rights require that the state protect innocent human life.

Neither Hohfeld nor Kelsen probe human rights as such, yet we see that the duty principle applies to human rights as well: *A human right becomes a legal right only when it correlates to a legal duty upon the state to guarantee the right.*[9] For example, A's human right to privacy entails some duty on the state—such as to refrain from interfering with A's privacy, to protect A's privacy from interference by other parties, and so forth. To the extent that they are reliably enforced, duties that the state owes to individuals limit the powers of governments. The broader those duties are, and the more effectively they are enforced, the less despotic the state can become.[10]

TREATIES: FROM ASPIRATION TO LAW

As I noted in chapter 3, the modern system of states, or nation states, emerged in Europe in the sixteenth and seventeenth centuries. Those processes also witnessed the birth of modern international law. However, well into the early twentieth century states commonly observed international rules with the proviso of maintaining their national sovereignty. They considered themselves bound by an international rule only insofar as they had consented to it; and in practice even that consent could often be disregarded or withdrawn with few consequences.[11]

Many legal experts doubted whether it made sense to speak about international "law" at all. Of course, consent certainly plays a decisive role in ordinary legal systems, as when we enter into a contract or sign a will. And, as we have seen, early modern and Enlightenment social contract theories aimed to justify law by placing it on a foundation of collective consent. In practice, however, law binds us to many rules whether we consent to them or not, such as rules prohibiting murder or theft. If a domestic legal system were to apply only on condition that each of us had consented to be bound by it, legal systems would be difficult if not impossible to achieve. But much has changed over the past century. In today's world, in which countless transactions take place across borders every day, according to highly complex rules that do largely work, no one seriously doubts the existence of international law as such.[12] Yet it is more reliable in some areas than others, and human rights count among its most precarious branches.

From the moment that the Universal Declaration was adopted, those elements of sovereignty and consent were already impeding the development of a general system of international human rights. Recall also that, before that time, the ways in which governments treated their own citizens were ordinarily assumed to be a matter of domestic concern. Any concept of "international human rights" would have been self-contradictory. Either a matter was concerned with human rights, and therefore beyond the purview of international law, or it was concerned with international law, and therefore unrelated to human rights.

International law works well when governments incur few burdens and reap great advantages. For example, virtually all countries have joined the Universal Postal Union, which originated with the 1874 Treaty of Bern, as well as the 1944 Chicago Convention on International Civil Aviation. Even the most corrupt states profitably and therefore willingly participate in those arrangements. By contrast, abusive governments perceive human rights as bringing loads of burdens with few advantages. They dislike attention being drawn to their violations, and commonly persecute journalists and shut down civic organizations in order to avoid negative publicity.[13]

Even when states give formal consent to respect human rights, they constantly breach rules with impunity because they are big powers or are allied to big powers or power blocs.[14] By the 1950s governments showed little interest in the Universal Declaration, and yet it revived in the 1960s and 1970s, in part through anti-colonial liberation movements, but perhaps also because of a renewed internationalism, born out of a declining faith in capitalism, socialism, and traditional religious orthodoxies.[15] Internationalists started to push for stronger recognition of human rights as legally binding upon all states.

Yet sovereigntism was still strong, so a key pathway would become the more prudent, consent-based route known as treaty law. Strictly speaking, treaties are voluntary, binding only on states that agree to be bound by them, although we will see in a moment that things are not so simple. But to start, it helps to know that treaties (also sometimes called "covenants" or "conventions") come in many forms. First, some treaties are time-limited while others are intended to be permanent. Time-limited treaties may serve practical tasks, such as building a cross-border railway. Treaties intended to be permanent include, for example, those adopted to create the European Union. Second, some treaties, like those of the EU and other regional trading blocs, limit the number of participating countries, while other treaties are open to all countries. Following those two criteria of time limitation and member limitation, we see that the leading international human rights treaties strive to be universal in the broadest sense: all states are eligible to join, and the treaties are not time-limited. There are several ways in which states can become bound to treaties, but to keep the discussion from becoming too technical, I shall simply speak about states that "join," "sign on," or "become parties" to treaties.[16]

When work began in the 1960s to translate the Universal Declaration into treaty law, questions arose as to whether all the declaration's norms ought to acquire legal status. Given the problems of state consent and the weakness of international enforcement, some observers would have preferred a modest list containing only the most important norms: less ambitious and therefore more workable. But which norms would count as the most important? Experts have certainly questioned whether some of the

Universal Declaration rights can be called essential, such as employees' rights to paid vacations (Article 24). But those types of borderline rights are rare in the declaration. Most of the interests it covers would be hard to view as unimportant. Disputes about designating only a few rights as the most important soon broke out, echoing Cold War schisms.

Some specialists within Western democracies maintained that only classical, Enlightenment-era civil and political rights ought to count as fundamental human rights, as set forth in Articles 3–21 of the Universal Declaration. These included, for example, rights to fair trials, religious freedom, protections from torture, and equal treatment before the law. These experts believed that social and economic needs for food, clean water, health care, education, or employment could be met only by states governed according to principles of a civil society subject to government accountability and the rule of law.[17] For other observers, particularly from socialist and developing states, such an approach seemed rigged to cement Western supremacy, creating standards that would cast non-Western states in a perpetually negative light. They insisted that social, economic, and cultural rights, as set forth in Articles 22–26 of the Universal Declaration, ought to enjoy equal or greater status.[18]

To grasp that Cold War standoff, recall that, for example, in some U.S. states racial segregation was still widely intact, which, in turn, entrenched gaps between rich and poor, powerful and powerless, privileged and outcast. According to many partisans of social and economic rights, such inequalities cast doubt on whether citizens of Western nations, particularly the United States, could seriously be said to be enjoying human rights at levels higher than in many non-Western states. Soviet peasants may still have been eking out a living, but in the United States many descendants of slaves, sharecroppers, or Native Americans hardly lived much better.

The compromise struck at the UN was to separate those categories of rights into two treaties. The first category was to be covered by the International Covenant on Civil and Political Rights (ICCPR), the second by the International Covenant on Economic, Social and Cultural Rights (ICE-SCR). Both documents were completed in 1966, leaving countries free to become parties to either or both. Other major human rights treaties have included the 1948 Convention on the Prevention and Punishment of the Crime of Genocide (Genocide Convention), the 1965 International Convention on the Elimination of All Forms of Racial Discrimination (ICERD), the 1979 Convention on the Elimination of All Forms of Discrimination against Women (CEDAW), and the 1984 Convention against Torture and Other Cruel, Inhuman or Degrading Treatment or Punishment (UNCAT or the Torture Convention). Note also that those UN-based treaties were further supplemented by regional systems, namely, the Council of Europe, the Organization of American States, and the African Union.[19]

Most of those treaties served to flesh out norms that had already been stated in the Universal Declaration,[20] and to create monitoring procedures, yet we do also witness advances beyond the declaration. For example, in the 1989 Convention on the Rights of the Child (CRC) we find that states parties must "respect the right of the child to freedom of thought, conscience and religion," and must "respect the right of the child to freedom of association and to freedom of peaceful assembly." That idea would have been hard to sell to the mid-twentieth century world, and is not easier in much of the world today.[21]

Again, it is easy to attract nations to multilateral treaties when their governments see immediate, tangible benefits. Admittedly, in the long term, respect for human rights can certainly be said to enhance states' domestic prosperity. A population that is well treated is more likely to become prosperous and productive.[22] But those benefits are a mixed blessing for repressive governments, since improvement of basic life conditions tend to empower citizens over time, and empowered citizens are more likely to question and to challenge established political authority. Any government that wants its people to become prosperous, while remaining dictatorial, is fated to become highly repressive of individual freedoms.

Many governments sign up to human rights treaties knowing that monitoring procedures are weak, often as public relations exercises or to attract aid or trade. Today, even the most repressive governments have incentives for donning internationalist garb.[23] Recall, moreover, as Stanton, Douglass, and Anthony showed, that even a country's purely formal adherence to rights gives activists a basis for holding their governments to account and a rallying point to promote greater respect for rights.[24] Demanding human rights may be persuasive, but demanding human rights that a government has already agreed to implement, either via domestic law or via international law, is more persuasive. Despite the lack of strong enforcement mechanisms, international norms can lend ethical stature to dissenters in repressive states.

With that brief summary of treaty law in place, we can now appreciate some of the processes that distinguish human rights as a justice system. First, various goods or interests are identified as essential for all individuals everywhere, at least within the contemporary, postindustrial world. Second, in becoming a party to a human rights treaty, a state consents to incur internationally established duties corresponding to those goods or interests, even if it does so insincerely, as a public relations exercise. Yet many countries have joined such treaties. Given that high degree of at least formal consent, some experts might puzzle over my initial assertion that international human rights do not yet exist *at all*. According to standard doctrine, once states incur duties to protect the various Universal Declaration goods and interests, then those goods and interests become the objects of human *rights*: Hohfeld's and Kelsen's duty principle has been observed, and human rights have been created irrespective of states' original motives for joining in.

Certainly with respect to any rights and duties arising from the aforementioned treaties on postal delivery or civil aviation, the standard doctrine is correct. Rights arise under those treaties because states agree to incur the corresponding duties. But the argument I shall continue to develop is that human rights, which are meaningful only insofar as they are held and acted upon by individual citizens in pursuit of their essential goods and interests, are not so easily constituted as the foregoing textbook account of treaty law would have us believe. In addition to the duty principle, a discursive principle—a principle of free speech—will become equally foundational.

However, a bit more background into the international systems will still be required before I can introduce that element.

CUSTOMARY LAW AND RIGHTS CONSCIOUSNESS

Treaty law is not the only channel for human rights to become internationally binding. International, regional, and domestic courts, and many governments, have widely accepted that human rights also form part of *customary* law. Customary law binds all countries, including those that have not formally agreed to be bound by it. Norms become customary law when they acquire overwhelming endorsements from states and international organizations. For example, more than 150 nations have joined the 1948 Genocide Convention, which has also been widely endorsed by international organizations.[25] So those states are formally bound under that convention to refrain from committing acts of, or conducive to, genocide.[26] Yet that broad endorsement has, in turn, created customary law prohibiting genocide, binding even upon states that are not parties to the Genocide Convention.[27] Exactly which other rights form part of customary law has been debated, but experts in the field widely agree that a good number of the Universal Declaration's rights would be included, not least because the ICCPR, ICESCR and other leading treaties similarly boast high numbers of participating nations.

To recap: first, the Universal Declaration's original drafters undertook to agree on basic norms in principle, through that aspirational, nonbinding document. Second, diplomats and experts then started down the cautious path of the consensual, sovereign model by promoting treaties. And third, widespread adherence to those treaties, as well as other evidence of state and international policies and practices, has promoted a customary law of human rights, which formally binds states even if they have not given consent to be bound. So even the purely formal success of the major treaties strengthens the stature of human rights in customary international law.

Yet customary law is a strange beast. In one sense, it is the oldest form of law, dating back to when law was wholly or largely unwritten, and deeply embedded in broader ethical norms and practices. Certainly, customary law still arises within postindustrial nations. For example, national courts may look to prevailing customs within a given profession in order to settle a dispute. However, in most contemporary states the complexity of law demands volumes of written sources for their domestic legal systems, such as statutes and printed contracts. By contrast, the ongoing problem of states resisting human rights means that customary law plays a crucial role. It revives a very old form of law where we least expect it—not in some remote village, but in a global society that claims to encompass all nations and to embrace fundamental ethical principles. Sovereigntists are likely to distrust the major human rights treaties all the more, despite their officially consensual character, given treaties' propensity to generate nonconsensual, customary norms. Customary law starts to look like creeping globalism, which if not curbed today will overrun nations tomorrow. By contrast, for the internationalist it becomes hard to fathom what a country loses through globally binding human rights. It becomes hard to understand how a population overall would suffer simply because its government is criticized for, or impeded from committing, genocide, political repression, engineered famines, police brutality, mass torture, and other grievous violations.

Customary law points toward a pervasively globalized regime, particularly given the scope and importance of human rights. Today, a state committing gross abuses would readily be held in violation of international customary law even if it had never joined a single human rights treaty or made any commitment to human rights. In discussing actual or hypothetical situations, I shall continue to draw examples from rights generally recognized and grounded in the Universal Declaration, which I shall continue to refer to collectively as the "international human rights corpus" or, for shorthand, the "international corpus." However, I shall argue that my view about the relationship between human rights and free speech obtains regardless of whether we assume a broad or narrow list of rights. For example, if I cite rights to health care within a hypothetical scenario, which some readers would exclude, then the basic point I am making still stands, even if those readers prefer to mentally substitute that right with another one.

That interplay of treaty law and customary law, and of an intricate network of international, regional, and national systems, elicits another feature of human rights, which we could call their *systemic redundancy*: between treaty and customary protections, and between national, regional, and international protections, we find high degrees of repetition and overlap. For example, European democracies today include basic protections of civil rights and liberties within their national laws. At the same time, they have joined the European Convention on Human Rights, and are also parties to the ICCPR, ICERD, CEDAW, and UNCAT, which include similar protections. In addition, they are subject to international customary law, which again includes those same protections. Admittedly, any two human rights bodies may not interpret a given right identically, so there can be cross-fertilization; yet many a human rights professional would welcome more streamlined systems, not least because such intricacy renders human rights opaque and remote.

Yet internationalists also welcome systemic redundancy as a shield against sovereigntism. If genocide, mass torture, or other gross and systemic abuses represent heinous ethical breaches, then repetition of those norms at a variety of levels and within a range of organizations and institutions seems at worst to be a minor evil, and at best to stem from a powerful system of ethical as well as legal confirmation of human rights. Human rights operate not only in legislatures and courtrooms, but through the dissemination of the idea that all individuals are rights holders. Systemic redundancy helps turn rights from "on paper" formulas to widespread expectations. The stronger rights consciousness becomes, the greater the pressure on governments to respect rights.

One exchange between two scholars dramatizes the role of rights consciousness. In his 2014 book *The Twilight of Human Rights Law*, the conservative legal scholar Eric Posner explains a well-known skeptical view. Posner rehearses familiar criticisms that human rights are expressed in excessively general terms, enshrined in treaties and declarations that have limited force, and impose Western solutions on non-Western cultures. Posner views human rights as a diversion from the crucial task of identifying opportunities for economic investment and development on a country-by-country basis. He uses examples of violations worldwide to show that human rights law "has failed to accomplish its objectives."[28] As an example, he cites the disappearance in 2013 of Amarildo de Souza, a Brazilian brick-layer who was arrested by police in an operation to round up drug traffick-ers, and then subsequently disappeared. A public outcry later resulted in investigations and prosecutions of a number of public officials, reflecting broader concern about arbitrary and violent policing methods. But for Pos-ner, that incident proves that international norms had no concrete impact, even though Brazil has signed on to several international human rights treaties.

The veteran internationalist Dinah Shelton takes Posner to task. "Oddly," Shelton writes, "Posner's description of events suggests at least some success in enforcing the norms." Shelton observes that on Posner's own account, "public pressure led to the arrest of ten police officers who were charged with [Souza's] torture and murder."[29] Posner sees failure because no fool-proof international response was available to provide redress. Although Shelton, like most human rights professionals, candidly acknowledges those sorts of flaws within the international norms and orga-nizations, she argues that human rights also work through less tangible, more sociological, consciousness-raising processes.

Shelton challenges Posner for omitting any "discussion of what led to the public pressure." She points out that it was "in part the human rights law that is incorporated into the Brazilian legal system and widely known throughout the country." Shelton suggests that "such awareness and invo-cation of human rights might have given the public a legal basis for insist-ing on the investigation, prosecution, and punishment of the perpetrators that took place."[30] For Shelton, then, human rights contribute to a public consciousness that, far from standing outside human rights law, has always formed a crucial part of its operation.[31]

THE COSTS OF RIGHTS

Recall the aforementioned Cold War controversies about classes of rights: some experts from Western states insisted on the primacy of civil and political rights, while advocates of socialist or social-democratic models argued that economic, social, and cultural rights should enjoy equal or greater status. That debate was never just about rights, but about conflicting economic-political models, for the most part capitalist versus socialist.

The debate was often cast as a showdown between so-called "negative" and "positive" rights. Classical, Enlightenment-era civil and political rights, such as protections from torture and arbitrary killings, religious freedoms, or a free press, were often presented as "negative" or "hands off," and therefore low-cost. They were described as rights "to be let alone," free of undue incursions into our individual freedoms. The state, it was said, does not need to provide goods or services in order to protect those rights. It only needs to refrain from arbitrarily killing, torturing, obstructing free speech and religious observance, and so forth. These rights were also described as preliminary conditions for civil society, which must be in place if legitimate decisions about social, economic and cultural policy are to be made. On that view, only civil and political rights could seriously count as higher-order rights.[32]

In line with that assumption, economic, social, and cultural rights were seen as requiring commitments to deliver goods and services en masse, incurring the high costs of a comprehensive welfare regime. Traditionalists therefore viewed economic and social interests not as higher-order rights at all, but as long-term legislative and policy goals. They did not necessarily oppose social welfare, but believed that such programs could succeed only within a political system that was transparent and accountable. Meanwhile, advocates of social and economic rights claimed the opposite: an inclusive and effective civil society could not emerge until bellies were full, illnesses treated, families housed, and basic education provided.

Yet experts have long cast doubt on such rigid divisions between classes of rights. For example, it has been observed that economic and social rights need not always impose high costs. There have been instances in which governments actively sought to weaken political rivals by blocking food shipments or agricultural production, or by engineering famines and supply shortages.[33] In those cases, economic and social rights did not require expenditures. They could have been respected cheaply and "negatively," simply by leaving people to farm and trade as they had always done. Those governments would have had no grounds for blaming their failures to respect social and economic rights on high costs. Similarly, water purification, agricultural fertilization, immunization, and other measures can help to fulfill social and economic rights at low cost, and even the costs of public education promise returns on investment through a more skilled workforce.[34]

It has also been observed that the risks to public health caused after the explosion of the Chernobyl nuclear power plant could have been avoided at low cost if free speech had been protected in the Soviet Union, allowing scientists to voice their longstanding concerns openly and honestly.[35] Similar claims have been made after China punished experts who attempted to warn about COVID-19.[36] Meanwhile, just as economic and social rights are not always costly, nor are civil and political rights always cheap. For example, protections from torture, along with freedom of religion, fair elections, and other civil and political rights do not merely require restraint and inaction. They demand that the state ensure fair and efficient investigations, well-trained and well-equipped police forces, competent prosecutions for violations, independent and impartial administrators and judicial officials, genuine channels for review, adequate conditions of detention, and so forth, which all add up to a hefty price tag.[37]

According to the ICESCR, a state's duties extend only "to the maximum of its available resources, with a view to achieving progressively the full realization of the rights recognized in the present Covenant." That proviso means that social, economic, and cultural protections correlate only to "relative and progressive" duties upon states, dependent upon their available resources.[38] When the ICESCR was being drafted in the 1960s, socialist and developing states saw that clause as a buffer against criticism, but for nations facing financial constraints, as most do, it also applies to civil and political rights. In terms of cost, the difference between the ICESCR and the ICCPR is not all or nothing, not expensive versus cheap, but a matter of degree. Moreover, note that even during the Cold War, opinions did not divide strictly along geopolitical lines. Some Western democracies had built successful social welfare states, although they required economic prosperity in order to do so.

It is also worth noting that when the ICCPR and ICESCR were being drafted, five separate classes of rights—civil, political, social, economic, and cultural—were formidable enough for a world largely unfamiliar with the idea of international human rights. Since that time we have witnessed further expansion, such as the introduction of a sixth class of "solidarity" rights. These are not individual rights but rather collective claims among large populations, including rights to peace, environmental protection, or economic development, and in particular place burdens on wealthy and powerful nations. These proposed rights have also sown divisions. While many experts endorse such goals, some argue that the larger the corpus of human rights, the less weight any right carries. They worry that expansion leads to dilution. Some fear that the concept of a right becomes vacuous when it is used to advocate interests other than individual claims.[39] As mentioned, my aim in this book is to revisit the concept of a human right regardless of one's preferred corpus, so for now I shall continue to focus on rights commanding greater consensus.

Human rights impose costs, then, across the board. It was simplistic to call civil and political rights "cheap" and economic, social, and cultural rights "costly." Having said that, it would be equally simplistic to treat all rights as imposing equal costs. While some essential social and economic needs can indeed be met at low cost, the fact remains that, for most nations, to ensure high levels of all social and economic rights entails great expenditures, with ramifications for taxation and other economic policies. Today even economically prosperous nations boasting strong human rights profiles often struggle to fulfill all social and economic rights to a high standard.[40]

TRADE-OFFS

In 1993, with dozens of states queuing up to become democracies, a World Conference on Human Rights gathered to adopt a comprehensive summation of the movement, known as the Vienna Declaration and Programme of Action. Like the Universal Declaration, the Vienna Declaration is not a treaty and has no binding status. Yet it has commanded considerable authority, notably for its oft-quoted "indivisibility" principle, which runs as follows: "All human rights are universal, indivisible and interdependent and interrelated."[41] In some cases, rights do admittedly appear to be inter-related. For example, James Nickel observes that due process rights "support equality rights by blocking some manifestations of racism in criminal trials."[42] Yet in other cases the logic seems strained. For example, someone's right to food could in principle be fulfilled by a government that has violated that person's religious freedom, so it becomes hard to grasp how those two rights would be indivisible.

In practice, the indivisibility principle seems to have two meanings. First, it seems to denote a "loose" indivisibility, reflecting the view that a state's good performance on only some rights cannot suffice to fulfill the conditions of human dignity envisaged by the Universal Declaration, as long as other rights are neglected. A full belly makes one a healthier person, but does not fully satisfy the conditions of one's humanity, for which respect of other rights is required as well. Second, even if questions remain about the character and extent of interrelationships between rights, leading monitoring bodies accept a related "non-subordination" principle: throughout thousands of reports published over decades, what emerges is that all Universal Declaration rights are deemed to be equally important. No official report has ever suggested that any human right ought to be subordinated to any other. Building in a bit of flexibility, we might find some modifications—recalling again doubts about whether some rights, such as rights to paid vacations, genuinely stand on a par with other human rights. But such modifications would be slight, since most Universal Declaration rights are not of that type. Accordingly, monitoring bodies have suggested that, in principle, no state should prioritize some rights above others.

The problem is that under circumstances of financial constraint even states acting in good faith must make choices about the extent to which they will respect particular rights. Their spending priorities inevitably translate as choices between different human rights. The candid term for such choices would be "trade-offs," yet it is testimony to the official sanctity of the non-subordination principle that the reports of monitoring bodies studiously avoid any such suggestion. Consider a 2018 report by the UN Committee on Economic, Social and Cultural Rights on Mali, one of the world's poorest nations. The committee acknowledges Mali's "security, climatic and poverty-related challenges," but then expresses concern "about the limited mobilization of domestic resources to finance programmes aimed at realizing economic, social and cultural rights."[43] A similar approach recurs in many reports on poorer states. Such reports certainly avoid overt condemnation. However, we must still wonder what, exactly, is being recommended, beyond the open-ended platitude—which would apply to *any* contemporary state—that Mali should somehow just try to perform better.

Often government officials are corrupt and pocket public funds. But even if we exclude problems like political incompetence or corruption, we are forced to draw an inconvenient conclusion. Most states can protect some human rights only at the expense of others. The indivisibility or non-subordination principles are sometimes naïvely recited as if human rights were *not* zero-sum, but any cost-imposing regime is by definition zero-sum, even on the assumption that respect for human rights supports economic growth. Greater funds for sanitation in a schoolroom means less money for prison hygiene; greater spending to ensure fair trials means less to monitor police brutality, and so forth. In a word, *most states can protect some human rights only by neglecting other rights*. Over coffee in New York or Geneva, human rights professionals freely confess that they make trade-offs by overlooking some violations in order to focus on others. Precisely because most states are forced into trade-offs, human rights professionals must informally acquiesce. Again, as mentioned earlier, contemporary doctrine certainly does refer to the precept of "relative and progressive" duties, but never has that doctrine been officially acknowledged to entail necessary trade-offs of rights. The official doctrine is non-subordination: no one right is more important than others. The unofficial doctrine is that some rights are always placed above others. That gap between the theory and the practice of human rights is wide.

In any world of limited resources, it is not the principles of indivisibility or non-subordination, but the opposite, the principle of trade-offs, that becomes essential and constitutive of human rights. Whether one views a trade-off performed by a particular state as having been done in good faith often depends on one's politics. When China curbs individual liberty while promoting economic growth, its supporters attribute good faith on grounds of overall public prosperity; its detractors attribute bad faith on grounds of bogus security rationales. When American legislation limits basic protections for low-paid workers and the unemployed, while cutting taxes for high earners, supporters attribute good faith on grounds of free-market principles, while detractors attribute bad faith on grounds of social justice.

Note that the principle of trade-offs does not strictly contradict the principle of non-subordination, but does give it a new meaning. If no one right ranks above any other, *then any trade-off becomes as valid as any other* (perhaps with the exception of the most extreme abuses, such as genocide). A state can indifferently, and justifiably, devote resources to any rights r_1, r_2, and r_3 while neglecting any other rights r_4, r_5, and r_6. My task in the next chapter will be to show why that quintessentially managerial stance remains altogether antithetical to any idea of a human *rights* regime.

* * *

In this chapter I have summarized some of the main features of contemporary human rights. In the twentieth century, theorists like Hohfeld and Kelsen contributed to identifying what I have called the duty principle, which defines a distinctly legal concept of a right by correlating it to some legal duty. Accordingly, a human right counts as a genuinely legal right only when it correlates to a legal duty carried by the state. However, the problems surrounding rights arise not only from concepts and definitions, but from institutions. International human rights first emerged within a deeply sovereigntist world, which explains much of the complexity surrounding their piecemeal development, including the complicated interweaving of treaty and customary law, and the surplus of international and regional monitoring bodies, often overlapping in their tasks.

That complexity certainly has its drawbacks, as it risks making human rights appear incomprehensible for the ordinary person. Yet on a positive note, it can be added that the proliferation of human rights systems—systemic redundancy—has promoted global rights consciousness. Still, a further institutional problem remains, namely that international monitoring bodies officially refuse to acknowledge the reality of trade-offs. They insist on the indivisibility or non-subordination of human rights, yet economic realities compel them to practice the opposite. They tacitly acquiesce in trade-offs, thereby abandoning the principles of indivisibility and non-subordination.

5 THE MOST HUMAN RIGHT

Recall from the last chapter the state of Regalia. Its dictator Bruder holds the power to bind all other citizens through law, yet remains unbound by any law. Regalia protects various interests appearing in the Universal Declaration, including religious freedom, ample food, comprehensive health care, anti-discrimination policies, prohibitions on torture, and humane conditions of incarceration—but only as a matter of discretion, through acts of benevolence. Now assume that Regalia has joined the International Covenant on Civil and Political Rights (ICCPR) and the International Covenant on Economic, Social and Cultural Rights (ICESCR). It has done so not because it accepts any correlative duties, but as a public relations stunt.

Under international treaty law Regalia's government is now formally bound to a great range of human rights. Most experts would argue that even without signing up to those Covenants, Regalia is bound to many of the rights they contain under customary law. Still, Regalia's domestic law imposes no duty to offer those protections. Some experts will insist that, by actually delivering some of those goods, Regalia fulfills all correlative duties under international law, regardless of its domestic arrangements. Many will say so out of sheer pragmatism: as long as the duties are being fulfilled, let's not get too preachy about legal niceties. Yet the fact remains that Bruder can and does sometimes grant and retract such goods at will, so any international duties exist for Reglia solely on paper.

Regalia is important because many nations in history and still today resemble it. Regalia casts doubt on whether the concept of human rights has any meaning at all, aside from states merely delivering goods that are rhetorically called rights. Again, we are assuming that Regalia delivers such goods equally or better than many states that do formally accept human rights as duties. UN monitoring bodies will simply follow their established procedures, holding Regalia to the same criteria as Norway or New Zealand. Regalia will probably be judged more critically than those two, but so are the United States and most other nations. Given the aforementioned unspoken doctrine of necessary trade-offs, a monitor's report on Regalia is unlikely to read much differently than reports on most other nations, and may well look better than those of some democracies.

From the perspective of such monitoring bodies, what distinct role, aside from a rhetorical one, does the concept of international human *rights* actually play? How does it differ from the sheer fulfilment of checklists of goods? The monitoring bodies will, so to speak, assess Regalia's volleyball performance, just as it assesses the volleyball performance of every other state, even though, in word and deed, it is playing ice hockey. In other words, they will judge its human rights performance even though it very clearly does not accept any serious, non-rhetorical conception of human rights. It does not accept any conception of human rights *as* rights. Should we care? As long as the people of Regalia enjoy a fair number of human goods, and don't seem to complain very much, does it matter whether they enjoy them as human rights? Is it all just semantics? Doesn't the true activist care about the immediate needs of "real" people "on the ground," regardless of whether we use the term "goods" or "rights?"

In this chapter, I shall argue that there is an unbridgeable chasm between, on the one hand, managerial regimes of goods and, on the other hand, citizen-directed regimes of rights based on free speech within the public sphere. Regimes like Regalia can certainly be assessed according to criteria of human goods that render human rights superfluous. But if that is all the monitoring bodies are doing, then they should say so candidly. The Regalias of this world cannot seriously be assessed according to human *rights* criteria at all.

RIGHTS AS CLAIMS

Throughout thousands of reports of major monitoring agencies, published over decades, it becomes clear that some states are certainly criticized more harshly than others. Yet even states with strong records are always found to require improvements, largely as a way for monitoring bodies to demonstrate their political impartiality.[1] These bodies certainly take into account circumstances that may make human rights more difficult to respect for disadvantaged states, such as poverty, foreign military invasions, widespread domestic unrest, or natural catastrophes, yet the rights themselves remain as fixed criteria. Norway is criticized for inadequate performance of rights r_1, r_2, and r_3; Russia is criticized on rights r_4, r_5, and r_6, and so forth.

The report about Russia may turn out to be harsher, but that is the only difference. The template is one-size-fits-all, which most internationalists would defend as necessary to ensure even-handedness. The nonsubordination principle, together with the tacit assumption of necessary trade-offs, means that the only difference between Norway and Russia is a difference of degree. According to official monitoring practice, the only difference between them *as* human rights regimes is quantitative, not qualitative. Current international practice leaves us bereft of any criteria for judging that that Norway fundamentally *is* a human rights regime while Russia fundamentally is *not* one. Nor indeed is that the kind of qualitative distinction that leading international organizations ever draw.

Again, a given monitoring body might certainly issue a report critical of Regalia. For example, one of its concerns might be to urge Regalia, within its own domestic law, to take more seriously its duties under international law. Perhaps the report will also recommend that Regalia allow greater political participation, political protest, and other such freedoms, assuming that these tend to be curtailed in dictatorships. Yet those sorts of criticisms scarcely differ from reports issued every day about UN-member states. The report on Regalia may turn out to be relatively mild compared to states that formally claim to accept human rights treaties but then massively violate them. So we face a paradox: rights presuppose duties, and Regalia acknowledges no such duties, yet Regalia seems to deliver goods set forth in the Universal Declaration and other treaties better than many states that *do* acknowledge the duties. Regalia can perform better than many other states through an entirely managerial regime of goods.

So what distinct meaning do human rights even hold *as* rights? Hohfeld points us toward a reply. He ventures that if we "seek a synonym for the term 'right'" in its specifically legal meaning, "perhaps the word 'claim' would prove the best."[2] Once again, Kelsen reaches the same conclusion. For Kelsen, some particular conduct is imposed as a legal duty upon any given party "as the content of a 'right,'" that is, "as the object of a 'claim' [*Anspruch*]."[3] What do they mean by describing a right as a claim? It seems that two qualities distinguish a legal right: first, as we have seen, a legal right entails a duty; and second, a legal right presupposes opportunities to make claims for that duty to be performed.

As an aside it is interesting to note that Hohfeld's English word "claim" can be traced back to the Latin *clamare*—to call, cry out, or clamor. Kelsen's German word *Anspruch* links to *sprechen,* which means "to speak." Yet the word "claim" can have various meanings. I can claim that the moon is made of cheese. What Hohfeld and Kelsen have in mind is that a legal right entitles us to *lay a claim* to something. The American legal philosopher Joel Feinberg (1926–2004) develops that point. Suppose Bill owes Diana $20,000. As Feinberg explains, anyone can *claim that* the $20,000 ought to be paid to Diana, but only Diana (or Diana's representative) can, through a legal procedure, lay a *claim to* the $20,000.

When Diana is chatting to neighbors over the fence, claiming that Bill owes her $20,000, she is only describing a particular situation. But when she declares in court, "Bill owes me $20,000," she executes what Feinberg calls "a legal performance." Once one lays a *claim to* something in law, that action "can itself make things happen."[4] Feinberg argues that the difference "between *making legal claim to* and *claiming that* is that the former is a legal performance with direct legal consequences whereas the latter is often a mere piece of descriptive commentary with no legal force."[5] He adds, "The legal power to claim . . . one's right or the things to which one has a right seems to be essential to the very notion of a right."[6]

Yet this case of *Diana v. Bill* does not yet seem to prove very much. The range of free speech required for Diana to lay her claim seems rather narrow. Bill may even acquiesce by paying the amount due without litigation. What matters, however, is that Diana's claim presupposes that such litigation always remains as a background defense of her right. Even for that ordinary rights claim, it remains true by definition that an individual legal right presupposes a sphere of speech at least free enough for the claim to be fully articulated. Surely Hohfeld and Kelsen failed to explore that point because it would have seemed too obvious to belabor. Moreover, the scope of speech required to litigate *Diana v. Bill* might seem narrow, but might suddenly balloon if Diana can subsequently introduce evidence that Bill had committed bribery, that the judge was biased, that the trial was unfair, and so forth.

The next step will be to apply those observations to human rights. But before doing so it is important to emphasize that the speech presupposed by rights can take various forms. If a corrupt judge rules in Bill's favor, Diana may mount her soapbox and decry the outcome in a public park, assuming a regime in which she enjoys that freedom. That "soapbox in the park" stands as an archetypal image of free speech, although few of us have ever done it. Nowadays our soapbox often takes the form of an online posting, with the "park" being a social media site, although live street protests are still alive and well. Yet even those various types of speech by no means exhaust the range of free speech presupposed by the pursuit of a right. For example, in a more everyday case, all Diana ordinarily needs to do is to fill out some forms. She may hand the entire lawsuit over to an attorney, without directly speaking on the matter at all.

However, even those standard processes are nothing but communicative steps aimed at securing Diana's rights. Filling out forms is a mode of communication. Hiring a lawyer makes sense only if the lawyer enjoys the full freedom of speech required to pursue the legal claim. Assume that Bill heads up a mafia, which intimidates Diana and her attorney to prevent them from filing or otherwise pursuing the claim, and which also bribes officials to prevent them from protecting Diana. In that case, she cannot pursue her claim because the necessary channels of communication are blocked. But then shall we say it is not free speech but rather public safety that is required as a precondition for the existence of rights—and, for that matter, food, water, health care, and the like, which seem equally necessary if Diana is to pursue her claim?

Consider the following objection of one legal philosopher: "The fact that one has a claim . . . does not entail that one must be able to assert that claim in the form of speech. Perhaps the legal system has a procedure whereby you file your 'claim' but do not do anything else. If such claims are respected, it is not clear that the entitlement to a claim . . . does require speech."[7] Here too, however, to file a claim is to engage in communication by notifying authorities that one is seeking satisfaction of the claim. What that writer might have in mind is a society in which government would always satisfactorily respond, so that free speech would be at most a trivial component of a right. Filing a claim would be like pushing a button on a coffee machine. The right would be fulfilled with the same clockwork mechanics that coffee is dispensed.

The problem is that in such a scenario the concept of a right loses any specific meaning. The performance of rights now merely collapses into the delivery of goods, with rights ceasing to play a meaningful role. If a system of rights, as a means of obtaining goods, is to maintain any distinct character, it can only be via claims *as* tools of communication. Certainly, adequate food, water, public safety, or health care are essential if we are to pursue our rights, but only in the obvious sense that they are essential to *any* means of obtaining essential or desired goods, be it under a democratic rights regime, a medieval monarchy, a theocracy, a military junta, or a technocratic dictatorship. Only free speech is distinctive of how goods are obtained by means of rights. Rights differ from other means of obtaining goods insofar as individuals stand not only as beneficiaries of goods, but as active agents in the procurement of those goods. Active human agency means communicative agency. Active agency in the pursuit of essential or desired goods presupposes free speech. Rights exist because we cannot generally assume that essential or desired goods will be delivered with the ease of pressing a button.

One might object further that there was no reason why Hohfeld and Kelsen *had* to use the word "claim" (*Anspruch*) in order to explain how rights work. As the same writer argues: "Suppose we use the word Schmaim"—in other words, a specially concocted token word with no historical or etymological connection to speaking—"for the idea that you have an entitlement to something and must be able to assert or demand its fulfillment." According to this line of thought: "A person with a Schmaim must have a process by which she can demand the fulfillment of the right but [that process] need not take a speech-like form." However, the concept of "speech" in law has only ever been shorthand for all forms of expression and communication, including nonverbal. So there is no such thing as a "demand" that "need not take a speech-like form." If Fred Flintstone bangs his club on the table while pointing at a bronto burger, "demanding" it without speaking, that nonverbal gesture is still communication,[8] just as waving a peace sign, burning a flag, or organizing a silent vigil is communication.[9] There is no sense in which one can "demand"—or urge, request, advise, entreat, beseech, or admonish—"the fulfillment of the right" without performing a communicative act.

THE DISCURSIVE PRINCIPLE

Everyday conflicts about ordinary rights are often of the *Diana v. Bill* type. Within reasonably well-functioning legal systems, they presuppose communication, though rarely of the controversial kind that would raise questions about the role of free speech. Even courts within repressive dictatorships can often resolve such cases, insofar as the speech involved is routine and poses no risks or challenges to the government or to other powerful institutions. By contrast, the sheer range of interests covered by the Universal Declaration means that human rights must necessarily presuppose a vast sphere of free speech. Moreover, in the world of human rights, the relationship between a *claim to* and *claiming that* radically changes. Suddenly *claiming that* involves a great deal more than chatting over the fence. As we have seen, human rights are pursued at many levels, and not entirely, or even primarily, through fully-fledged judicial processes. Changes in popular consciousness can bring results, and popular consciousness is influenced by *claiming that*. It may start with a chat over the fence today, but then snowball into a grassroots movement tomorrow.

There is no single best way to pursue human rights, given their content, scope, and the endless cultural contexts in which they arise. Sometimes the best option may be a courtroom, sometimes an appeal to administrative officials, and sometimes a petition to legislators. So an ancient question surfaces: *Quis custodiet ipsos custodes?* Who is to guard those guardians? How are the accountable to be held to account? What recourse remains for individuals who believe, rightly or even wrongly,[10] that legislatures, courts, or agencies have failed to protect their human rights? That ultimate recourse, after all else has failed, can rest only with the individuals themselves, through their freedoms to dissent, to mobilize, to campaign—in a word, to speak. In Kant's words, free speech remains "the sole palladium of the people's rights."[11]

Individuals must maintain a broad freedom to protest existing interpretations of rights, and to propose that new rights be introduced, or that interpretations of established ones be changed or expanded. I only have a human right to a fair trial, to humane conditions of detention, to health care, and so forth, if I can openly protest that such rights have been denied to me, or if others can do so on my behalf. I must maintain that prerogative even if my rights have not been denied, which, as demonstrated by cases like *Dred Scott*, *Bradwell*, or *Plessy*, is often more a matter of interpretation than fact. *Human rights correlate to state duties, but also to the possibility of publicly scrutinizing the interpretation and performance of those duties within a safe and robust sphere of public expression.* For the rest of this book I shall refer to that condition as the *discursive principle* of rights, which stands alongside the duty principle as an essential ingredient.[12] Of course, "safe," "robust," "public expression," and "free speech" itself are wide-open terms, to which I return in chapter 6.

It does not suffice merely to argue, as countless writers have done, that free speech is *helpful* for human rights. After all, recall that the indivisibility principle holds true in a loose sense: the protection of most rights does in some sense *help* the protection of others. I certainly do need to eat, and I benefit when I have decent housing. Both of those can be essential if I wish to agitate effectively for my rights. So I am not saying that observation is incorrect. Rather, I am saying it is too correct by half. It holds under virtually any justice system. It tells us nothing about what distinguishes human rights. Moreover, in many systems, ancient and modern, some opportunity to speak would *help* people to pursue justice; many traditions boast internal networks of consultation, but "consultation" leaves ultimate control in the hands of superiors as to who will be consulted, and when, and about who speaks for whom. Human rights become indistinguishable from managerial regimes of goods when individuals lack access to a safe and robust public sphere. It is true that many other belief systems share values appearing in the Universal Declaration. However, if that fact only means that various managerial systems overlap in the goods they recognize, then nothing has been proved at all about those systems' compatibility with human rights. Such overlap becomes possible only through the discursive principle.

In a famous pronouncement, the Nobel Prize-winning economist Amartya Sen wrote that "no substantial famine has ever occurred in a country with a democratic form of government and a relatively free press."[13] Sen uses the example of a famine not to distinguish food from other human goods, but as one example of any number of goods—health care, education, and so forth. He observes that efficient management of human goods depends on the ability of citizens to hold their governments to account. Yet even that justification for free speech remains instrumental and outcome-based. In other words, if famines could be averted, and indeed other goods and interests protected without free speech, which surely is possible in principle, then free speech would prove to be *non*essential to the pursuit of human rights. Sen very rightly correlates free speech to human rights, but that is still too little.

Other writers, too, have argued, as an empirical matter, that free speech correlates to better human rights performance.[14] However, in so doing, they leave open the possibility that we could one day find a non-democracy performing well on many goods covered by the international rights corpus. The evidence cited by those writers certainly adds some support to the discursive principle, but my point is that the discursive principle holds not simply as a matter of observation, but as a matter of definition. By definition, even states performing well on the delivery of human goods are in no way providing human rights if they are failing to guarantee a safe and broad public sphere of free speech.

The discursive principle joins the duty principle as a coequal precondition for the existence of human rights. The sequence works as follows. First, under the duty principle, a human right correlates to a state duty. Second, only the discursive principle guarantees the individual's exhaustive pursuit of that human right. Any serious and distinct meaning of "human rights," unlike the concept of "human goods." must inherently include the possibility of openly pursuing them.[15] Earlier I suggested that the discursive principle must apply irrespective of the human rights corpus one prefers. Imagine, then, a very small corpus, limited only to a few of the most traditional civil and political rights. Is a general freedom of speech still required? Would one need any great freedom to speak about food or housing? Yet that is why I am arguing that citizens' prerogatives to pursue their rights must include the prerogative to advocate expanding or reinterpreting the existing corpus.[16] As *Dred Scott*, *Bradwell*, and *Plessy* remind us, today's far-fetched demand may become tomorrow's imperative, whether we are talking about interpretations of existing rights or the introduction of new ones. I could scarcely agitate effectively for a right to some adequate level of food if I were barred from citing and critically discussing examples of malnutrition.

Certainly, starving people may care little about the difference between goods and rights, between managerial regimes and rights regimes. But if we think that what matters is not only what people get, but also their empowerment to get it; if we think it matters whether citizens can become political agents, and whether goods are to be actively pursued or only passively administered, then the difference becomes primordial. Looking back at history, there is no doubt that delivery of some goods to some people improved in the USSR under Stalin or in China under Mao. Both Stalin and Mao could rhetorically acknowledge their states' "duties" to do so. But in no sense were those goods provided as a matter of individual right, even when the rhetoric of rights was at times energetically recited in international forums, as it is by autocracies today.

Why has the discursive principle gone unnoticed? Answers are certainly imaginable, but can become complex. For now I'll try to summarize them in a few paragraphs, before moving on. Again, an individual legal right presupposes a sphere of speech free at least large enough for the claim to be fully and fairly adjudicated, yet since writers like Hohfeld and Kelsen failed to explore that condition, their readers might easily have ignored it; or some may have come away with the opposite impression, namely, that the free speech component is secondary. Readers might have surmised what experts generally *have* surmised: that a legal system may certainly contain a free speech right, but that such a right by no means stands prior to other rights as the necessary condition for rights *to be* legal rights.

For example, in 1980 the philosopher John Finnis published *Natural Law and Natural Rights*, an attempt to found higher-order rights upon what Finnis described as certain essential characteristics of human beings. Finnis adopts Hohfeld's analysis without qualification[17] yet accords no primary role to free speech. Other writers have followed Finnis in that respect, even when adopting very different approaches. A few decades later, James Griffin's 2008 work *On Human Rights* departs from Finnis's method through greater engagement with existing international systems, but otherwise maintains the conventional conception of a human right with no particular attention to speech.[18] In their defense, one might argue that their models assume a two-step procedure: if the right to free speech were inadmissibly infringed, then an individual could first litigate that right before litigating some other right. But then that sequence would only confirm that free speech does stand as a prior or simultaneous condition for the pursuit of other rights.

In *International Human Rights*, Jack Donnelly and Daniel Whelan employ Hohfeld's terms to define a right, without citing Hohfeld—a testimony to Hohfeld's influence. In their words, when we assert that "A has a right to *x* with respect to B," what we mean is that "a right holder (A) stands in a special relationship to a duty-bearer (B) with respect to the object of A's right (*x*)."[19] Yet they, too, do not proceed to examine the "claim" aspect, or its consequences for free speech. Unlike Finnis, whose six-page discussion of Hohfeld incorporates the strictly analytic tradition of Hohfeld, Donnelly and Whelan write as political scientists. They aim to synthesize a broad range of historical, political, and institutional materials on human rights without anchoring them to any fixed definition. In that respect, they resemble scholars like James Nickel[20] and Charles Beitz.[21]

Again, human rights professionals are inclined to argue that free speech is necessary to make claims only in the sense that food, clean water, and any number of other rights are also necessary; however, Hohfeld and Kelsen were never examining "necessity" in that sense, but only in terms of the possibility of an individual legal right existing at all. They, too, would certainly have agreed that a full belly helps when one must appear in court; yet, returning to Hohfeld's quote above, when he writes that "the word 'claim' would prove the best" synonym for "right," his notion of a claim *conceptually* presupposes communication. It presupposes communication *by definition*, in a way that it does not presuppose even essentials like food, water, protection from torture, or even a fair trial, except insofar as trials consist largely of speech. Those goods become rights only on the condition that free speech has already become a right.

FROM FREE SPEECH TO DEMOCRACY

Yet if autocracies can deliver many of the goods promised under international law, then can't one of those goods be free expression? It is true that various empires and monarchies—Chinese, Persian, Roman, Bourbon, Japanese, Prussian, Hapsburg, Ottoman, and others—have at times known liberal periods, where expression was relatively free. And, again, non-democracies throughout history have certainly maintained consultation networks for learning about people's needs and wishes. Still, a sphere of public discourse cannot provide a foundation for human rights when government retains a discretionary power to grant free speech today only to penalize the speaker tomorrow.

If the first condition for existence as a human being is life, then the first condition for existence as a citizen is speech. Many factors may legitimate a state as a state, but only a protected sphere of public discourse legitimates it as a democracy. For example, refraining from torturing prisoners, guaranteeing fair trials, or avoiding famines are all policies that lend legitimacy to a state *as* a state. They count as perfectly good steps toward democracy, if that destiny lies on the horizon, but none of them suffices to render a state democratic. A state does not need to be a democracy in order to torture less or to assure access to food, which is surely one reason why most justice systems throughout history have not presupposed democracy. Food and water are required for a democratic society to thrive, but only because they are required for *any* society to thrive.

So what is distinctive about democracy? One response might be that people are free, but free in what sense? Free to trade? To practice their religious beliefs? To choose sexual partners? To own and use firearms? To consume hard drugs? Like "justice" or "fairness," "freedom" can mean many different things. But then what else might be distinctive of democracy? Another popular reply is that citizens can vote. Yet voting is done in a few minutes out of the year. My question is not what makes us democratic for those few minutes, but what makes us democrats all day, every day, and the only answer is: free speech. Even voting is nothing but a formal procedure for speaking. Curiously, in most Germanic languages, the words for "vote" and "voice" are the same, as in the German *Stimme*, the Dutch *stem*, or the Danish *stemme*. The English "vote" traces back to the solemnity of pledging or "vowing" (*vovere*).[22] Even voting derives from something more foundational, something constitutive of it. It is not different from speaking; rather, it is an exemplary type of speaking.

The notion that only democratic procedures lend legitimacy to political processes and outcomes, procedures including freely and fairly contested elections, is a time-honored one. In the optimism of the post-Cold War years, Thomas Franck argued that norms imposing democratic legitimacy on *domestic* political processes formed part of *international* law.[23] I appreciate that Franck's argument lends some support to mine, but it does not go far enough. It is based on the state of international law and institutions at a particularly optimistic moment in history, but that perspective is too tentative. Human rights presuppose democracy by definition, and not only when political winds happen to be blowing the right way.

The kind of democracy I have in mind could never be a crudely *majoritarian democracy*, whereby even a decision to arbitrarily kill off some minority would have to be adopted as long as it commanded a numerical majority. One aim of contemporary human rights regimes is to avoid that result. That is also an aim of contemporary *constitutional democracy*, a term used to refer to institutions established in order to avoid such abuses of government powers. A broadly constitutional democracy is required, whereby a citizen may speak even if every other citizen objects to the message, just as many may object to a—seemingly—far-fetched rights claim. The claim may fail, but, in a human rights regime, ongoing chances to pursue it must remain intact. Various types of regimes may grant greater or lesser freedoms of speech, but only in a constitutional democracy can a fully-fledged sphere of free speech count as foundational.[24] So the logic can be stated succinctly: *Human rights presuppose a constitutive sphere of free speech, and a constitutive sphere of free speech presupposes constitutional democracy. Therefore human rights presuppose constitutional democracy.*

Now imagine another state called Democratia, which maintains a safe and robust sphere of public discourse but has a poor record on, say, criminal justice, racial discrimination, and health care. Democratia qualifies as a constitutive, albeit defective, human rights state insofar as it ensures a possibility for individuals to publicly claim human goods *as* legal rights. Again, the standard practice of international monitoring bodies is to admonish Democratia for its performance on rights r_1, r_2, and r_3, just as they admonish Regalia for its performance on rights r_4, r_5, and r_6. Placing those reports side by side, there may be no obvious way of comparing the two states overall. Regalia may end up looking better.

Again, for most internationalists, the idea that Democratia and Regalia are held to the same standards would confirm the system's fairness. In fact, it proves the death of international human rights, or rather that they were never really born. Regalia is not a defective human rights performer in the way Democratia is. To see Regalia as "defective," alongside any number of other states, each differing from the others solely as to the particulars of their violations, is to commit a category error. That error has nevertheless stood as the uniform practice of international organizations and experts. Their motives have been laudable—to bring nations into the fold, to promote human rights through an ethos of inclusiveness, to avoid assertions of Western domination. But Regalia does not present an alternative conception of human rights, or an alternative means of achieving them. It is not a defective human rights state, but a *non*-human rights state. It may deliver human goods, but does not offer them as human rights. It does not render human goods available through the fully-fledged pursuit of legal rights. Any purported performance by authoritarian regimes of human *rights* is not merely imperfect, but self-contradictory. It makes perfect sense to place Norway and the Kim dynasty's North Korea on the same scale to assess their delivery of human goods, such that North Korea merely ends up receiving the lower grades. However, to place them on the same scale to assess their performance of human rights is to collapse any difference between human goods and human rights, and to destroy any distinctly legal concept of a human right. That is how the concept of human rights becomes empty rhetoric.

There is no such thing as a state performing well or poorly with respect to a regime that it does not have and is not set up to have, except in the obvious sense that a report might say about Putin's Russia, Xi Jinping's China, or Erdoğan's Turkey that they simply do not have human rights. As mentioned, I can take my seat in the stadium, and can report on the skill with which the players skate around the court and shoot the puck into the goal. But I have no basis for assessing how well they are playing volleyball, because they are playing ice hockey. Or consider another analogy. We could only meaningfully call a hamster a poor zebra hunter if hamsters were structurally, anatomically, constituted to hunt zebras. Hamsters do not present a "defective" or "alternative" means of zebra hunting. The difference between a lion and a hamster is not that the hamster merely has a further road to travel toward zebra hunting. To assess a lion as a good zebra hunter and a hamster as a poor one is to reduce zoology to diplomacy and anatomy to rhetoric, in order to keep the hamsters on board.

On a generous reading, Regalia governs as a paternalistic steward of goods, as many governments throughout history have done, often with popular approval. If that is all we seek, then we have no need for human rights. The concept then becomes empty, and we should stop misleading the world by constantly invoking what we have turned into meaningless verbiage. Nations like the United States, India, or Brazil certainly can and should be called defective human rights performers. Through procedures supported by reasonable (though far from flawless) channels for free expression, they are in principle set up to perform human rights even if they protect many rights poorly. Their failures cannot be equated with those of nations that, by comprehensively repressing speech, are not set up to perform human rights at all. Even if Putin's Russia, Xi Jinping's China, Erdoğan's Turkey, or Khamenei's Iran do provide important human goods, by definition they fail to provide them as human rights. The contemporary international regimes were designed to avoid such a result by presenting human rights as politically transcendental, or indeed as apolitical, applicable to all regimes irrespective of their politics. But that ideal contradicts itself. There is no such thing as a system of substantive norms that are both constitutive of all politics and yet magically apolitical. Insofar as human rights presuppose democracy, they categorically demand certain types of regimes and exlude others. The possibility of human rights constitutively excludes non-democracies.

Again, pragmatists or activists may have little patience for such distinctions between rights and goods. Some might reply: "It makes no difference to me whether you say 'goods' or 'rights.' My concern is with helping people on the ground, here and now." Far from eschewing philosophy, that response defaults to a philosophy of its own, as pragmatic stances often do. The philosophy it assumes is that we must seek to ameliorate inferior human conditions wherever possible, without wasting time on conceptual niceties. I certainly have no objection to that position, but then we need to be frank about it. It only supports my argument that the prevailing concepts of international rights are readily exchanged for concepts of discretionary goods with no change in meaning.

Unlike other critics, I am not proclaiming an all-out assault on the UN. I acknowledge that it is a multifaceted organization that performs many tasks, some more competently than others. Nor am I reiterating the old complaint that the current international regimes are impractical or ineffective. I recognize that the discursive principle may appear utopian for the simple reason that the most repressive states will never adopt it. But that objection, too, only confirms how readily internationalists have substituted human rights models with managerial ones, however benign their intentions may be. The notion that states are unlikely to adopt the discursive principle should come as no surprise. It is germane to any serious and detailed justice theory that it must embrace high standards, which regimes cannot easily achieve. The rapid and widespread recognition of the international corpus throughout the decades following the Universal Declaration should certainly have lifted our hopes, but should also have raised some red flags. With the best will in the world, the international community has downgraded human rights to the moral equivalent of free beer offered to undergraduates on condition that they attend a ten-minute lecture by a retiring dean about the virtues of cheerfulness. The price is so low that there is little incentive *not* to sign up. Yes, the proliferation of human rights standards has promoted a greater global consciousness, but a human rights system needs more.

Some will call it unrealistic to expect a state to maintain strong protections for free speech before basics like food and housing are in place, but in adding the discursive principle to the duty principle, I do not have any strictly chronological sequence in mind. What kinds of interests ought to take priority in any given place or time can be controversial. Whether or for how long a managerial model may be required before a human rights model can be implemented is equally controversial, although "impracticality" is history's age-old trump card to avoid ever taking action. Stanton and Anthony were constantly told that their cause was sound, but too hasty. Douglass was constantly told that African Americans should have equal rights, but it wasn't yet time. Opponents of South African apartheid heard the same. Imagine that Putin's Russia or Erdoğan's Turkey were suddenly to introduce vigorous protections of individual free speech, ensured through genuine democratic norms. They would then become human rights regimes, not least because, leaving aside customary law, both have signed up to more than enough treaties, so their purely formal duties are already in place. But nothing short of such a transition would be required. When a government prioritizes other interests above free speech, that simply means that, rightly or wrongly, it declines to establish a regime of human rights. Whether that choice is defensible is a separate question, and plenty of people are on Putin's and Erdoğan's side.

DEMOCRATIC DILEMMAS

Again, if we were to ask what "democracy" means, some might reply that it is a system in which citizens may stand for office and cast votes, but others would mention that it is a system that protects individual rights. Notions of democracy and individual rights have become so deeply interwoven that we often speak about them as if they denote the same things.[25] Yet the relationship has always been fraught. As we read in every textbook, we inherit the concept of democracy from the Greek *dēmokratía*, meaning "rule by the people." Classical Athens sheds light on that history because by ancient standards it was a vibrant democracy, yet lacking any concepts of higher-order rights, which, as we have seen, emerge only in systematic and at least quasi-legal forms during the Enlightenment. When an assembly of several hundred citizens voted in 399 BCE to sentence Socrates to death, they did so by majority vote. He had no higher-order rights to protect him. (What was Socrates' crime? "Corrupting the youth" by challenging their beliefs in accepted Athenian ideas. Today we would call it a speech crime.[26])

Democracy as such does not presuppose human rights, but human rights do presuppose democracy—or rather, constitutional democracy. Yet now the problem is that once we face a corpus of rights as expansive as the Universal Declaration, skeptics start to object that almost none of a society's major social concerns can be decided democratically, since human rights largely decide them, often handing them from elected legislatures to appointed judges. Given the costs and in some cases the large state apparatus that is required to implement many rights, the fear is that we will end up with an ever-growing state coupled with ever-shrinking democratic controls over it. The internationalist would reply that it is hard to imagine what kind of democratic process would still be required for us to conclude that torture, unfair trials, and other violations of the Universal Declaration are morally wrong and so these are limits on democracy that strengthen democracy.

Some fear that an exhaustive regime of higher-law rights creates precisely the overweening state from which rights were supposed to free us. Once again, that fear does not divide neatly between "negative" and "positive" rights. As we see in the United States, for example, efforts to secure abortion rights or to promote LGBTQ+ rights spark fierce resentments in those who doubt the higher-law basis for those rights and believe that they must therefore be decided in the democratic arena. Within many international organizations, LGBTQ+ rights, although still often resisted, have posed less of a problem because they have been easier to ground within existing human rights texts.[27] By contrast, various bodies have pushed human rights law to the limit in arguing for high standards of maternal care and family planning, but abortion rights, which would cause backlash from many governments, have not yet been incorporated into international human rights law.

It seems, then, that two axes centrally concerned with the existence, content, and interpretation of rights are closely linked. Table 5.1 illustrates relationships between the axis of sovereigntism versus internationalism, and the axis of pro-rights versus anti-rights regimes. A pro-rights state admits higher-order individual rights as limits upon government powers, and even upon laws enjoying majority support. Accordingly, some sovereigntists, as shown in box 1, favor rights but only insofar as they are determined and interpreted nationally. By contrast, other pro-rights voices assign a decisive role to international law, as reflected in box 3. Even for box 3, what is important is that international procedures are designed to supplement domestic ones, and not to supplant them. International regimes would work best when strongly supported by domestic law, which is the usual expectation. In box 1, international law would have no such complementary role to play.

An anti-rights state precludes any role for higher-order individual rights that might override government powers. In that case, no human rights system exists in practice at all, even if one has been adopted or agreed on paper. If all such powers are concentrated in the state, then, as suggested in box 2, the regime is autocratic. Finally, some states consent to be bound by international law in areas that reap material benefits under globalized travel, trade, or military alliances, but not in the area of human rights. In box 4, I classify them under what could be called "laissez-faire internationalism." Table 5.1 does not summarize all possible political models, but focuses on those that can be meaningfully described with reference to its axes of pro- versus anti-rights, and sovereigntism versus internationalism.

Democracies take their place along a spectrum. At the anti-rights extreme, a democracy becomes nothing but brute majoritarianism. At the opposite extreme we find a regime of rights so extensive that the terrain of democratic decision-making risks ending up consigned to secondary problems, speaking at best only peripherally on important political or ethical ones. Ironically, some will find that regime, too, exceptionally managerial, but as long the discursive principle operates for individuals to pursue their rights, then such top-heavy administration, although clearly raising concerns about the democracies we want, does not jeopardize the human rights regime as such. Unsurprisingly, debates today focus more on which higher-law rights we should have and how broadly they should apply, rather than whether they should exist at all.

Table 5.1 Sovereigntist and internationalist perspectives on rights

	Sovereigntist	Internationalist
	1	**3**
Pro-rights Higher-order individual rights can legitimately trump certain government powers.	**Domestic constitutionalism** Higher-order individual rights are acceptable, but only as adopted and interpreted within domestic law.	**International human rights** Higher-order individual rights should be determined, monitored, and implemented through international institutions (not to replace but to supplement national systems).
	2	**4**
Anti-rights Higher-order individual rights cannot legitimately trump any government powers.	**Domestic autocracy** Law and policy, whether or not it is democratic, should be controlled by domestic government, without limitations imposed either through domestic or international higher-order rights.	**Laissez-faire internationalism** International relations may focus on travel, trade and military alliances, but without higher-order individual rights ascertained, monitored, or implemented through international law or institutions.

DEMOCRACY INDEXED

Does the world divide so tidily into democracies and non-democracies? Even across prosperous Western democracies differences in law, politics, and culture can be vast. You may have extensive knowledge about American democracy, but it will not get you far in understanding the Dutch or Japanese systems. According to which criteria, then, can a state be called sufficiently democratic to count as a state set up to perform human rights?

In 2006, the *Economist* launched its annual *Democracy Index* reports, designed to evaluate nations throughout the world.[28] The *Economist* has long led the media as an influential voice for values of free trade, largely as pioneered by the Anglo-American world. Some readers might suspect that the editors would award high marks to pillars of that world, such as the United States and Great Britain, dismissing the reports as mouthpieces of global capitalism. Yet the highest-ranking states have usually been social democracies with strongly redistributive economies. In some years, the United States has struggled even to gain a place within the upper tier of nations, which the editors label as "full democracies." Britain, less welfarist than the top-performing states but more so than the United States, has performed respectably enough, but has never ranked among the leading democracies. A few geopolitical pairings prove that the regional free-market hegemon does not necessarily impress the editors: Ireland repeatedly outranks the UK, New Zealand repeatedly outranks Australia, Canada repeatedly outranks the United States.

The editors avoid drawing clear lines between democracies and non-democracies. They propose a sliding scale, dividing countries into four types: "full democracies," "flawed democracies," "hybrid regimes," and "authoritarian regimes." In 2020, the distribution worked out as follows: 23 countries (comprising 8.4 percent of the global population) ranked as full democracies, 52 countries (41 percent of the global population) ranked as flawed democracies, and 35 countries (15 percent of the global population) ranked as hybrid regimes. A whopping remainder of 57 countries, ruling over more than one-third of the global population (35.6 percent), ranked as authoritarian. In order to arrive at those results, countries are ranked according to criteria such as "electoral process," "functioning of government," "political participation," "political culture," and "civil liberties." Those headings are open-ended and perhaps disputable as to particular countries, but my aim is not to scrutinize the findings in detail. I want only to note that there are workable criteria for identifying the societies in which citizens are or are not able to participate within public discourse in order to pursue their rights. In some years the *Democracy Index* has identified fewer than twenty states as full democracies.

Yet even if the editors have resisted a one-dimensionally capitalist governance model, does the report still end up with a Western bias? Given that human rights are not cheap, prosperous Western societies have enjoyed a competitive edge. However, the top-tier states have included Botswana, Cape Verde, Costa Rica, Mauritius, and Uruguay. Needless to say, "full" does not mean "perfect," so international monitoring bodies still find abuses within full democracies, as in *Q v. Denmark*. When an otherwise competent UN human rights body criticizes countries such as Norway and New Zealand, or even the United States, India, or South Africa, an argument can certainly be made that it is then performing a genuine human rights function, since these states have maintained at least reasonable protections of free speech in the public sphere.

Accordingly, leaving aside pragmatic questions about the difficulties of implementation, supervision, and enforcement, we can fairly say that international human rights regimes do exist for the small number of "full" and for some "flawed" democracies. In that respect I am happy to acknowledge that human rights have indeed been born within the domestic legal systems of a modest but respectable number of countries. However, for as long as Norway and North Korea are being assessed according to identical criteria, differing only insofar as Norway puts in a better performance, the birth of a serious international human rights regime remains far from view. One might argue that there was enough free speech for the Kazulin and Ernazarov cases to be brought, and to end up before the UN Human Rights Committee, despite the low annual *Democracy Index* rankings of Belarus and Kyrgyzstan. Following that approach, we might decide to look at each dispute case by case to determine how much free speech was possible. But that strategy would lead nowhere, not least because we would struggle to identify cases that were never brought due to censorship and other silencing tactics. Such cases are often pursued in non-democracies at great risk to lawyers, activists, or journalists who wish to call attention to them, and often include foreign NGO or expert assistance. Autocratic regimes commonly inveigh against such NGOs as foreign agents and infiltrators.[29]

The discursive principle would be difficult to promote because oppressive states would reject it, but also because the UN would reject it—and yet not for any pragmatic reasons. For example, the UN Human Rights Committee could easily divide states into one set of states in which free speech is sufficiently protected for citizens to pursue their rights, followed by a second set in which it is not, and perhaps a third, intermediary set in which the status of free speech is too difficult to ascertain. The committee could then issue genuine human rights reports on states belonging to the first set, while states in sets two and three would simply be assessed on their delivery of goods. In practice, however, such an approach would outrage many governments and perhaps even some experts who remain wedded to the current systems.

RIVAL MANAGERIALISMS

But do global economics favor the handful of liberal democracies that can maintain the luxury of free speech, which other countries can ill afford? That point touches on the debate between Eric Posner and Dinah Shelton that was mentioned in chapter 4. Posner speaks for many skeptics, arguing that international rights regimes ineptly combine Western values with clumsy interference in non-Western societies, producing few successes. Meanwhile, Shelton speaks for internationalists in responding that those regimes were never designed to work with the precision that we would expect from highly prosperous nations, and indeed have achieved more than he concedes. Joining Shelton is another veteran internationalist, Hurst Hannum, who takes Posner to task in similar terms.[30] What seems to emerge is a rather conventional "anti-human rights" versus "pro-human rights" debate.

Yet on closer examination it becomes clear that nobody in these debates is talking about human rights at all. Posner and his fellow travelers never actually assail human *rights*, nor do Shelton, Hannum, and other internationalists ever defend them. The interchangeability of human rights with human goods is glaring in Posner's case, since he makes no assumption that international human rights do have any distinctive meaning or importance. On his view, if torture and arbitrary detentions *can* be eliminated, then by all means; but if economic investment and development can best be promoted by ignoring those evils and directing investments toward roads and power plants, which he clearly considers to be the more probable scenario for many abusive regimes, then so be it.

Posner favors ad hoc micromanagement over comprehensive, internationalist macromanagement. I need to signal that I am using the term "micromanagement" differently here from how it is often used, simply to draw a clear opposition to internationalists' "macromanagement." By "micromanagement" I do not mean that Posner advocates outside experts seizing control of the everyday minutiae of governance, but the opposite—he seeks less globalist, more targeted involvement. My bafflement arises not from Posner's admiration for technocratic micromanagerialism as opposed to citizen-directed human rights. What astounds me is that such a decisive feature of his book, his candid reduction of rights to goods, is the one feature that not even his sternest critics have noticed, because they all share the same managerial view, differing only on their preferred forms. Posner's micromanagerialism does not pit an anti-human rights stance against internationalists' pro-human rights stance. All these experts are merely using the phrase "human rights" to disagree about different managerial models. All of them assume that if the current systems call themselves human rights systems, then they must therefore *be* human rights systems, and should then be evaluated as such.

Posner writes, "When human rights advocates try to help a country, their goal is to bring the country into compliance with rules—*fewer detentions, less torture, more free speech*—which do not necessarily advance the *well-being* of the citizens in the target country. . . . It might make more sense for Western donors to help a country build a reliable road system than to force it to abolish torture."[31] The suggestion that "well-being" is not advanced by people *not* being tortured is a curious one, though Posner presumably means something like, "The pressure doesn't work anyway." I noted Shelton's reply, focused on mass consciousness, in chapter 4, so I shall not further explore it here.

But to see how close the skeptics' micromanagerial position and the internationalists' macromanagerial position really are, let's take a closer look at Posner's examples: "fewer detentions, less torture, more free speech." We can take them in turn. First, as to "fewer detentions," Posner obviously means *arbitrary* detentions, and not detentions resulting from fair trials. More importantly, anyone can be subjected to arbitrary detention, perhaps through police error. In practice, however, gross and systemic practices of arbitrary detention are generally political, deployed to silence rivals and dissenters—that is, to limit free speech. Second, as to the example of torture, anyone can be tortured, but systemic practices of torture are mostly set up to prevent political opposition— that is, to limit free speech.

So Posner's view that we should not overly insist upon "fewer detentions, less torture, more free speech" translates into something simpler, namely, we should not overly insist on *free speech, free speech*, and *free speech*. It comes as no surprise that the ingredient Posner finds least worrying, the suppression of free speech, is the one that would turn human goods into the objects of human rights. That should have been the paramount and glaring omission that his critics would have pounced upon. As we have seen, no less than Posner, internationalists do informally concede that some rights must in practice take priority over others. So they all recognize free speech as "important," but no more so than other rights. It becomes a technical question whether we end up choosing Posner's micromanagerialism or Shelton's and Hannum's macromanagerialism. Shelton or Hannum might reply that they have always supported citizen empowerment, but the prior question is whether a regime exists in which such empowerment is even possible—that is, in which citizens can openly pursue their rights and criticize their governments' delivery of them.

Leftist critics, too, while purporting to critique international human rights, have only ever assumed managerial models of goods. For example, in a 2004 essay the political theorist Wendy Brown captures a number of contemporary leftist criticisms leveled against the international rights regimes. Brown recites familiar but fair warnings about abuses of the values and terminologies of human rights. For example, she recalls how the rhetoric of rights has been cited to justify violations committed by the United States in Afghanistan, Iraq, and Guantanamo Bay. She also links those abuses to more general concerns about the deployment of rights discourses to promote global capitalism.

Like many critics, Brown does not reject human rights per se. She claims to be open to human rights, albeit subject to "a left tilt."[32] Once again, however, we find a writer who at first seems to take issue with internationalists, but turns out merely to squabble with them about preferred managerial models. Brown seems happy enough with a regime in which "civil and political rights must be supplemented by . . . social or economic rights," but presents as her political ideal a regime that would "insist on the *primacy* of rights to food, shelter, and healthcare."[33] Like the globalists she criticizes, Brown tosses free speech alongside other rights, or rather subordinates them among the ranks of civil and political rights, thereby failing either to adopt or to criticize any distinct concept of human *rights* at all.

Many leftists, like many internationalists, do plausibly insist that no grassroots empowerment is possible without a bedrock of food, shelter, clean water, health care, and other social and economic goods. We must certainly take that view into account, since it is the reason many will doubt the primacy I accord to free speech. However, my disagreement with Brown is not that I assign primacy to free speech while she assigns it to social and economic goods. Rather, it is the same as my disagreements with everyone else. Brown simply is not talking about human rights in any sense distinct from age-old conceptions of managing human goods. Brown appears to presuppose a well-known sequence: first we accord primacy to social and economic goods, and then people can become equal and active citizens. Of course, there is a long history of regimes promising that sequence. At various moments in the histories of the Soviet Union, China, Cuba, and other socialist states we certainly find groups whose living standards improved. The associated politics served, however, not to create mass citizen empowerment but to suppress it entirely. Brown drops no hint about how her model would avoid that outcome. Again, even in prosperous and top-performing human rights states, voices arise routinely to the effect that redistribution has not gone far enough.[34] That being the case, Brown offers no clue as to the kinds of timelines she has in mind for poorer nations, or whether these can even be plotted out.

To be sure, like the other scholars, Brown would surely insist that free speech is somehow important, not least because she and they profusely avail themselves of it. Yet her preferred model ends up in the position that women or minority groups have faced for generations, this time running as follows: "Of course, free speech is important. But this is not the right time." In Brown's defense one might respond that she takes a position no different from mine: she seeks only the necessary, not the sufficient conditions of justice. In other words, meeting people's basic needs may not always lead to citizen empowerment, but still no one can become empowered without those needs being met. Many would agree with that formulation, but I am only pointing out that a justice system can easily prioritize people's material needs without needing a concept of human rights.

On a grammatical note, consider some ways in which Brown's position might be phrased. We might say: "People's material needs must first *be met.*" Then there are more active constructions, but only in the grammatical sense: "*We* must first meet people's material needs" or "*Governments* must first meet people's material needs." Whichever wording we adopt, that lexicon of the essential prior moment *before* individual empowerment, which would arguably require years if not decades, speaks the quintessential language of managerialism. By contrast, there is one sentence with which none of those sentences equates. It runs as follows: "People must have the means to make their demands for themselves." That formulation by definition places free speech before material demands insofar as those demands are to become objects of human *rights*. So I am not arguing that Brown's approach is necessarily wrong. I am only saying it is conventionally managerial, and could drop the reference to rights entirely without any change in meaning. The only difference between the foregoing positions is that Posner would steer the sheep to the right, Shelton would steer them to the center, and Brown would steer them to the left.

* * *

In this chapter I have set out my main argument. This book's aim is to ask whether human rights have any distinct meaning in contrast to many belief systems throughout history that, in one way or another, have promised various tangible or intangible goods. Legally binding human rights acquire that distinct meaning only insofar as they presuppose a vast and protected sphere of free expression within public discourse. I have called that the discursive principle of human rights, and it stands alongside the duty principle to define the essential components of a legally binding human right. Only constitutional democracies can ensure those protections, even if some of them fail to do so in practice.

The point is not that free speech is more important than essentials such as food or housing for survival or for prosperity, but only that free speech stands as a necessary condition if any human good is to become the object of a human right. States that fail to guarantee a safe and robust sphere of public discourse are not "defective" human rights states. They are not "poor" human rights performers. Rather, they are not set up to be human rights regimes at all, however well they may deliver some of the goods set forth in the Universal Declaration of Human Rights. To purport to assess their performance according to human rights criteria is to commit a category error. In failing to acknowledge the discursive principle, experts both favorable to and critical of human rights have collapsed what should have been citizen-directed regimes of human rights into managerial regimes of human goods. Consequently, the international concept of a human right has lost any distinct meaning, and merely equates with a human good.

6 DO ALL OPINIONS COUNT?

The scope of free speech within the public sphere must be vast if citizens are to have adequate opportunities to pursue their human rights, but how vast? Today, every major social problem somehow involves human rights. Do human rights therefore presuppose free speech absolutism? In this chapter, I shall consider some of the protections of free speech that are necessary for a human rights system. I shall borrow from some U.S. First Amendment disputes decided around the mid-twentieth century, along with a European Court case, mostly because these cases vividly illustrate some core free speech principles. Readers versed in the First Amendment will already know the U.S. cases, but the few examples I discuss are chosen solely to a sketch a basic notion of the citizens' public sphere, and not to offer any detailed recitation of free speech law.

We must also bear in mind that, contrary to popular opinion, and despite the strength of the First Amendment "on paper," the United States is by no means the nation most protective of speech in practice, as witnessed, for example, by its history of crackdowns on peaceful political demonstrations, often along racial lines. For example, in the 2020 *World Press Freedom Index* published by the independent monitoring group Reporters Without Borders, the United States ranked only 45th among 180 nations. In earlier years, too, the United States has failed to rank in the top tier of states, mirroring the *Democracy Index* findings and other studies.[1] I shall draw, then, from First Amendment doctrine, but I by no means place the United States as the global leader in its concrete governance of free speech.

We must start by asking what is meant by "speech." So far I have used the phrases "free speech" and "free expression" interchangeably, and will continue to do so. "Free speech" is the more usual phrase, but "free expression" is more accurate. "Free expression" certainly includes verbal speech, but also includes nonverbal messages, such as silent vigils, or displays of flags and symbols.

With that terminology in mind, the fantasy of "free speech absolutism" can be seen off in short order. If speech were absolutely free, there could be no penalties even for highly dangerous speech, including, for example, forms of fraudulent advertising. Labeling poison as a health tonic would have to be legally protected, since even a limit on speech based on public health grounds would still be a limit, meaning free speech would not be absolute. The state would have no power to prevent us from scrawling graffiti on each other's houses: a property-based limit, too, is still a limit. Indeed, since free expression includes nonverbal messages, I could justify breaking any law simply by asserting that I had wanted to send some symbolic message—for example, I had sped through a red light in order to express my free spirit; and then the next day I had ignited a forest fire in order to express my sense of *Weltschmerz*, and so on. Any absolute freedom of speech or action would undermine the very possibility of a legal system.[2]

Some might reply that they do not mean "absolute" literally, but rather something like the "greatest possible" freedom. But then "possible" according to which criteria? Debates about what counts as the "greatest possible" freedom have a long history. According to the 1789 French *Déclaration*, "Liberty consists in being able to do anything that does not harm others."[3] That idea was later famously explored by John Stuart Mill, whose essay *On Liberty* announced his famous harm principle: "The only purpose for which power can be rightfully exercised over any member of a civilized community, against his will, is to prevent harm to others."[4] Mill's harm principle has an initial appeal, because it seems that a good way to define abstract concepts is with reference to less abstract ones. "Liberty" being abstract and controversial, Mill attempts to define it via the seemingly more concrete concept of "harm." For example, the statement "I feel unfree" may sound vague and speculative, but the statement "I burned my finger when you pushed me into the fireplace" seems in principle verifiable. So while "liberty" presents disputable questions of value, "harm" would seem to present testable assertions of fact. Either I burned my finger or I didn't. Either you pushed me or you didn't.

But does Mill's harm principle work beyond those obvious scenarios? In the nineteenth century, empirical fact in the social sciences was thought to carry greater certainty than it does today. Yet, on closer inspection, it is inaccurate to suppose that "liberty" depends on value while "harm" depends on fact, or that the one term is more abstract, or less disputable, than the other. Both terms turn out to be steeped in controversial ethical values.[5] Some harms, like burning my finger, may be relatively concrete, but many are not. In the arena of free speech, controversies have raged about whether, for example, racist, sexist, homophobic, transphobic, ableist, terrorist, or pornographic speech, or fake news on matters of public concern, cause harm—and, if so, of what type and to what degree?

There is no precise way to name those very different types of speech. The term "hate speech" is commonly used to cover some of them, but I shall use the broader phrase "extreme speech."[6] *On Liberty* still often stands as authoritative, but it sheds too little light on contemporary controversies. Much of Mill's discussion speaks to his own time, when State and Church wielded strong powers to censor, for example, workers' rights rallies or publications deemed blasphemous. Mill never writes in detail about the crises of extreme speech that preoccupy us today, and attempts to apply Mill's thinking to our own controversies have led to contradictory interpretations. Some believe his harm principle compels us to accept extreme speech; others point to Mill's own qualifications to suggest that the harm principle is compatible with bans on such speech,[7] particularly in an age when social media have added to the power of such speech. In a word, Mill helps with the easy cases, not the hard ones. The concept of harm fails to provide clear guidance about extreme speech.[8]

Following U.S. First Amendment doctrine, another approach is to distinguish between the *content* and the *viewpoint* of speech. The content refers to the subject matter; the viewpoint refers to a particular stance *on* that subject matter. For example, bans on false advertising are content-based. They apply to everyone, irrespective of any given individual's ethical, religious, political, cultural, or other viewpoints. We can certainly imagine someone labeling poison as a health tonic for political reasons, perhaps to target members of some economic, racial, political, or religious group; however, the point of a content-based restriction is that this would be inadmissible under all circumstances, irrespective of whether it is undertaken to make money, or as a vicious prank, or pursuant to a particular ethical, religious, political, or other viewpoint. Other content-based restrictions include, for example, bans on courtroom perjury, bans on breaching confidentiality agreements between doctors or lawyers and their clients, and bans on defacing public property or others' private property.

By contrast, consider a ban on public demonstrations for LGBTQ+ rights. Assume that the ban does not forbid all demonstrations pertaining to LGBTQ+ people, but only demonstrations favoring such rights.[9] Now we have a ban that prohibits the expression of a particular ethical, political, religious, or cultural worldview. Indeed the same government may actively encourage demonstrations condemning LGBTQ+ people, or demonstrations that simply hail "traditional" or "family" values.[10] In the remainder of this chapter I shall argue that human rights presuppose not free speech absolutism, but something approximating what I shall call *viewpoint absolutism within the public sphere*.[11] In other words, human goods become the objects of human rights only under a legal system that protects the freedom to speak and to write publicly, without censorship or penalty imposed solely on grounds of the speaker's ethical, political, religious, or other viewpoint.

Again, the range of problems with which human rights are concerned is vast, but does that mean that even one's freedom to express *viewpoints* must be absolute? For example, consider a country that bans mockery of its king. Does such a ban undermine the kinds of speech that are necessary to individuals to pursue their human rights?[12] And yet it is of the essence of viewpoint absolutism that complex problems can never be tidily circumscribed. For example, some citizens may believe that the public funds for maintaining a monarchy would be better spent on improving human rights performance. Of course, one might distinguish between criticizing the institution and criticizing the person of the monarch, but such distinctions collapse in real-world contexts. Ordinary people dissatisfied with the office will often associate it with the officeholder, and all the more so if, say, the particular monarch is perceived as corrupt or extravagant.

It is in the nature of language itself that conceptual categories cannot remain hermetically sealed—at least not within the realm of human affairs. Take the statement "Blue is more beautiful than yellow." Let's agree that one should be free to say it. But is that freedom a necessary condition for pursuing human rights? And yet in some countries it may turn out that blue and yellow have become associated in the public mind with particular political or cultural viewpoints. Someone may wish to express a preference for a political party whose flag is blue because that party advocates human rights. Rarely can we draw fixed lines between those viewpoints that should and should not be protected for purposes of founding human rights, because we cannot fix the meanings of the words and phrases of ordinary language. Those associations of blue and yellow may not have been long established within the language. They may have popped up haphazardly, in response to suddenly publicized reports of government abuses. Nor can we strictly contain the elements that a particular human rights dispute may entail. For example, there would be no way of fully probing Ernazarov's abuse and death in prison without airing the broader problem of sexual taboos in Kyrgyz society. We cannot draw clear lines between those viewpoints that should and those that should not be protected for purposes of founding human rights, because we cannot foresee all possible links across social spheres that may arise within any particular human rights situation.

Or take the utterance "I prefer tea to coffee," which certainly expresses a viewpoint. Even the harshest dictatorships would have few reasons to ban such a statement, but do I need the freedom to say it in order to pursue my human rights? Imagine a strange regime that respects viewpoint absolutism on all possible topics of discussion, except that it bars people from expressing preferences for tea over coffee. Clearly, such a narrow restriction would not cause the regime to fail utterly as a human rights regime. And yet even here, it may be that some speakers would make such a statement because they believe that tea can more easily be produced in worker-friendly or environmentally sustainable ways, a standpoint that certainly does raise human rights concerns. What is crucial about viewpoint absolutism is that it involves no enquiry into our subjective motives for speaking.

What about freedom to denounce human rights as such, for example, as a decadent Western concept that does not really lead to justice? By definition, it would seem, one does not need that freedom in order to pursue one's human rights. Yet we read in the Universal Declaration that human rights include freedom of conscience (art. 18). As we have seen, some illustrious thinkers have rejected the concept of human rights entirely, or rejected the individualist assumptions about the human that human rights presuppose. On their own terms, human rights make sense only as a part of a system of justice, and the concept of justice makes sense only insofar as it is always amenable to proposals for greater justice, however controversial they may be. Even if we could argue persuasively that a proposed alternative would fail to deliver greater justice, we cannot ignore histories in which proposals for free speech or democracy, too, were deemed contrary to the demands of justice. Subject only to limits I shall discuss in the remainder of this chapter, human rights must protect anyone who, rightly or wrongly, argues for a system they believe to be superior to human rights.

Lines between content and viewpoint can also become difficult insofar as fact and opinion are not always easy to distinguish. For example, if I publicly name a particular police officer, whom I accuse of having violated my human rights, the accuracy of my statement may depend on intricate sets of facts. My charge may have serious consequences if, for example, the officer ends up dismissed or imprisoned. If it turns out that I lied, then the officer may rightly sue me for defamation and for the losses suffered due to my false accusations. In that case, my speech would be penalized on grounds of content, not viewpoint: any speaker who fails to back up detrimental claims about another individual may incur liability for defamation, irrespective of that speaker's political, social, or other viewpoints. And yet even questions about what counts as "detrimental" can become thorny, as some countries penalize legitimate dissidents through spurious defamation claims.[13] One useful criterion under U.S. law is the extent to which a targeted individual enjoys public platforms and concomitant opportunities to respond to or simply to overshadow false charges. For example, under U.S. law, prominent officials or those elected to high office can reasonably be denied the full protections against libel or slander that are extended to ordinary citizens on grounds that public figures have ample resources to influence information disseminated about them.[14]

FIGHTING WORDS

The phrases "public sphere" and "public discourse" are frequently used,[15] but hard to define. A first step can be taken by describing them in terms of what they do *not* mean. For example, not everything uttered in public places amounts to public discourse. Consider a vintage U.S. case. In April 1940, Walter Chaplinsky, a member of the Jehovah's Witnesses, stood in the Central Square of Rochester, New Hampshire, to distribute religious literature. Some locals became angry, in view of Jehovah's Witnesses' controversial beliefs, such as their refusal to salute the national flag. The New Hampshire Supreme Court later reported that the pedestrians had complained to the city marshal, who replied that Chaplinsky's activity was lawful. But then the city marshal turned to Chaplinsky to warn "that the crowd was getting restless and that he would better go slow." As the state court further reported: "Some hours later, the crowd got out of hand and treated Chaplinsky with some violence. He was then led by policemen towards the police station, though *apparently* more for his protection than for arrest."[16]

On the available record, the basis for that claim seems far from clear. The state court's equivocal language raises a question about whether Chaplinsky rightly feared he was being arrested for engaging in lawful activity. In any event, riled by the events, he exclaimed to the marshal: "You are a God damned racketeer" and "a damned Fascist and the whole government of Rochester are Fascists or agents of Fascists."[17] He was then arrested under a provision of a state statute that read as follows:

> No person shall address any offensive, derisive or annoying word to any other person who is lawfully in any street or other public place, nor call him by any

offensive or derisive name, nor make any noise or exclamation in his presence and hearing with intent to deride, offend or annoy him, or to prevent him from pursuing his lawful business or occupation.[18]

Looking back, we might wonder whether others present should also have been arrested for their violence toward Chaplinsky. We might also wonder whether, nowadays, we would expect senior public officials to grow thicker skins, and to accept that their roles may sometimes place them face to face with angry citizens. It is above all in non-democracies and flawed democracies that we would expect Chaplinsky to be penalized for what, today, sound more like angry than dangerous words. Be that as it may, the importance of this case lies not with those details, but with a more general principle set forth by the New Hampshire Supreme Court. While acknowledging the First Amendment's protections of free speech, the court upheld the state statute and Chaplinksy's conviction, observing: "The English language has a number of words and expressions which by general consent are 'fighting words' when said without a disarming smile." The court continued: "Such words, as ordinary men know, are likely to cause a fight. So are threatening, profane or obscene revilings."[19] Arguably, even if public officials can be expected to toughen up, our main concern would be about such insults hurled between private individuals.

On appeal, the U.S. Supreme Court upheld the New Hampshire decision, citing that passage.[20] It has long since entered the canon of First Amendment jurisprudence, known as the *fighting words doctrine*. Perhaps the word "likely" in "likely to cause a fight" is exaggerated, since there are many situations of everyday anger and aggression that do not lead to physical violence. Yet for the U.S. Supreme Court, physical violence need not be an absolute certainty before such speech can legitimately be penalized. As any bouncer in a busy urban bar or club will attest, many situations can spark violence before the actors have had a moment to cool off, and in ways too sudden for the police to arrive in time to defuse the situation.

The fighting words doctrine shows that public discourse does not include anything and everything that might be uttered in public places. The phrase's meaning lies not primarily in the word "public," but in the word "discourse," which suggests some prompting to discussion, even for those who decline the invitation because they find the speech offensive or provocative. Fighting words are the exception that prove the rule of free speech within the public sphere: in those kinds of hot and sudden street or barroom encounters, it would be far-fetched and possibly hazardous to assume that speakers are prompting the targeted individuals to engage in an exchange of ideas.

For now, I'll leave to one side speculation about how we might want a court to decide a case like *Chaplinsky* today. Be that as it may, a strong case can be made for applying the fighting words limit to a good deal of extreme speech. As I shall observe later in this chapter, the hardest legal problems arise with respect to extreme speech articulated in general terms to general audiences. But there seems to be little difficulty in agreeing that racist, sexist, homophobic, or other types of abuse directly targeted at particular individuals need not be legally protected. There certainly are a few purists who would insist that even that kind of invective should be legally protected, but my aim is not to contemplate in each instance what might be the ultimate outer limit of protected speech. I am asking only, in general terms, to what extent speech must be free to ensure that citizens can pursue their human rights. Any suggestion that one would need to personally target other individuals with racist, sexist, homophobic, or other such abuse as a necessary condition for pursuing a Universal Declaration right seems so fanciful that it need not be further explored here.

THE PUBLIC FORUM

What I am calling viewpoint absolutism in the public sphere derives loosely from U.S. First Amendment law, although the phrase itself is my own distillation, not one the Supreme Court has ever used. Whether the First Amendment today *can* altogether be called viewpoint absolutist has come into question,[21] and we would certainly be mistaken to assume the doctrine as a constant in American history. For example, anti-blasphemy laws were widely viewed as acceptable at the time the U.S. Constitution was adopted.[22] Only in the early twentieth century did a minority of Supreme Court justices begin to sketch something like a doctrine of viewpoint absolutism in the public sphere,[23] which a Court majority accepted only as recently as the 1960s.[24]

One case from 1949 illustrates how viewpoint absolutism would entail individuals' freedoms to speak provocatively on matters of public interest. Irving Feiner, a university undergraduate, addressed a large crowd gathered on a street corner in an African American neighborhood in Syracuse, New York. Feiner stood on a box, speaking through a loudspeaker attached to a car. He urged the mixed white and African American audience to attend a meeting of the Young Progressives of America to be held that evening. In so doing he availed himself of what might be called the quintessential *public forum*, which need not be a venue officially designated by the state.[25]

A permit to hold the planned meeting in a school auditorium had been revoked, so the meeting had been moved to a hotel, and Feiner was publicizing its new location while denouncing the initial ban. He branded the city's mayor "a champagne-sipping bum, who does not speak for the negro people." He called local politicians "corrupt," President Truman a "bum," and the right-wing American Legion a "Nazi Gestapo." He added what some might say was an incitement to violence: "The negroes don't have equal rights; they should rise up in arms and fight for their rights." Two police officers arrived, and initially looked on without interrupting Feiner. But onlookers grew restless. Some believed that Feiner, speaking to a mixed-race gathering, was aiming "to arouse the Negro people against the whites." One man complained about the police handling of the situation, telling officers that if they did not take that "S-O-B" off the box, then he would. When an officer told Feiner to get off the box, he refused and was arrested on a charge of disorderly conduct. In addition to creating a quintessential public forum, Feiner was engaging in quintessential *public discourse*. He had certainly provoked and offended some onlookers, but had spoken no fighting words—no insults targeted specifically at individuals present in the crowd. He spoke in general terms to a general audience.

In *Feiner v. New York*,[26] the U.S. Supreme Court upheld the state court conviction. The justices found that the police had rightly sought to control an unruly crowd. But today the case is remembered for the dissenting opinions of Justices Black and Douglas, who paved the way for the change of course the Court would adopt in the next decade. Justice Black protested that Feiner had "been sentenced to the penitentiary for the unpopular views he expressed on matters of public interest while lawfully making a street-corner speech."[27] Black rejected as "far-fetched" any suggestion that a bit of shuffling posed any "imminent threat of riot or uncontrollable disorder."[28]

In so doing, Justice Black sketched a contrast to speech-curtailing rationales, still ubiquitous around the world today, whereby governments recite grounds of "public order," "national security," "public safety," often with little or no evidence, for the sole purpose of stifling dissent—formally viewpoint-natural, but in practice viewpoint-selective. Note that Belarus prosecuted Kazulin under criminal laws prohibiting, in superficially viewpoint-neutral terms, "hooliganism" and "organization of mass events severely breaching public order."[29] Black continued, "It is neither unusual nor unexpected that some people at public street meetings mutter, mill about, push, shove, or disagree, even violently, with the speaker. Indeed, it is rare where controversial topics are discussed that an outdoor crowd does not do some or all of these things. Nor does one isolated threat to assault the speaker forebode disorder."[30]

Black denied that the sheer risk of disorder by incensed onlookers sufficed to warrant the police to silence the speaker:

> Assuming that the "facts" did indicate a critical situation, I reject the implication . . . that the police had no obligation to protect petitioner's constitutional right to talk. The police of course have power to prevent breaches of the peace. But if, in the name of preserving order, they ever can interfere with a lawful public speaker, they first must make all reasonable efforts *to protect him.* Here the policemen did not even pretend to try to protect [Feiner]. According to the officers' testimony, the crowd was restless but there is no showing of any attempt to quiet it . . . one person threatened to assault [Feiner], but the officers did nothing to discourage this when even a word might have sufficed.

Their duty was to protect petitioner's right to talk, even to the extent of arresting the man who threatened to interfere. Instead, they shirked that duty and acted only to suppress the right to speak.[31]

Regarding Feiner's slurs on the president, mayor, and local politicians, Justice Douglas maintained that extreme language is bound to enter the rough and tumble of open, candid speech: "When a speaker mounts a platform, it is not unusual to find him resorting to exaggeration, to vilification of ideas and men, to the making of false charges. But those extravagances . . . do not justify penalizing the speaker by depriving him of the platform or by punishing him for his conduct."[32] Such penalties would amount to placing police officers on the side of the offended listener, making the police "the new censors of speech."[33] Government's job is certainly to keep us safe, but too often that imperative translates as nothing more than officials' efforts to stay in power and to appease their consituencies. Genuine security threats may certainly arise, but under human rights law these cannot be recited willy-nilly. International human rights include the doctrine of "derogation," whereby certain rights (not all) may be limited or suspended during legitimately declared states of national emergency. Even then, the suspension may last only as required by the emergency, and only for as long as the emergency lasts, and must ordinarily be reviewable by an independent judiciary or some body independent of the government.[34] But again, these are formal criteria, which in practice governments often violate.

A decade after *Feiner*, the U.S. military was in Vietnam. In April 1968 nineteen-year-old Paul Cohen stood in the Los Angeles County Courthouse, where children were present, wearing a jacket emblazoned with the words "Fuck the Draft." He was convicted for "maliciously and willfully disturb[ing] the peace" through "offensive conduct," and sentenced to thirty days' imprisonment. Cohen fought his conviction to the U.S. Supreme Court, calling his jacket "a means of informing the public of the depth of his feelings against the Vietnam War and the draft." In *Cohen v. California* the Court agreed with him,[35] an important shift toward Black's and Douglas's earlier dissenting opinions. Throughout the 1960s many Americans had opposed and protested against U.S. intervention in Vietnam. No one seriously challenged Cohen's right to denounce government policy. Cohen did not just wish to express a position, but to express the passion behind it. Writing for the Court, Justice John Harlan noted that the state could not legitimately silence or penalize Cohen by construing such language as fighting words: "No individual actually or likely to be present could reasonably have regarded the words on appellant's jacket as a direct personal insult."[36]

Disagreeing with the Court, Justice Harry Blackmun would have sustained Cohen's conviction, calling the jacket an "absurd and immature antic" that was "mainly conduct and little speech."[37] That kind of view remains widespread today: "You're entitled to state your opinion, but you should do so in a respectful way," with the said "respect" often due to government. Or consider this version, which millions of people today would readily endorse: "A civilized dialogue is only possible with those political forces who put forward, justify and formulate their demands in a civilized manner and defend them within the bounds of the law." Those words were spoken in 2012 by Vladimir Putin, in a drive to weaken his political opponents under the guise of protecting Russian national and security interests.[38] The point is not to equate Blackmun with Putin, but only to underscore the risk that standards purportedly rooted in high-minded criteria of courtesy and politeness can easily degenerate into means of silencing rebellious speakers.

In response to Blackmun, Harlan insisted that once government starts down the road of regulating speech on grounds of taste and decorum, there is no obvious stopping point. Regulating the manner of expression solely because of the emotions expressed, however crude they may be, is nothing other than viewpoint-selective censorship: "the State has no right to cleanse public debate to the point where it is grammatically palatable to the most squeamish among us."[39] Harlan maintained that "much linguistic expression serves a dual communicative function: it conveys not only ideas capable of relatively precise, detached explication, but otherwise inexpressible emotions as well. In fact, words are often chosen as much for their emotive as their cognitive force . . . we cannot indulge the facile assumption that one can forbid particular words without also running a substantial risk of suppressing ideas in the process."[40]

Cohen betokens not only a change in law, but a momentous cultural shift. The democratic culture that forms the basis for human rights can exist only in a culture receptive to criticism of its own past and present. In parts of the United States today, school districts promote curricula that downplay slavery and Jim Crow, preferring history that glorifies over history that criticizes.[41] Yet students who are to become citizens learn by example. Only through critical approaches to past abuses do they learn vigilance about present ones. In many countries governments remain averse to the candid teaching of history, prioritizing naïve patriotism over critical thinking.[42] *Cohen* brings our journey full circle, back to chapters 2 and 3 where I recalled the essential individualism of human rights. In many places today there would still be popular support for convicting speakers like Feiner and Cohen.

Although the U.S. Supreme Court and European Court of Human Rights have not always treated free speech identically, they have certainly agreed on one idea essential to viewpoint absolutism in the public sphere: the state's first duty is to protect expression, silencing it only where danger is imminent with no other way to avert it. In 1980 a group of Austrian physicians organized an anti-abortion demonstration in a small town. The physicians were members of the organization Doctors for Life, seeking greater restrictions on the country's abortion rights. From the outset the participants were worried about hostility from counter-demonstrators. They raised their concerns with the police, hoping to receive adequate protection.

The physicians marched from the town cathedral to an altar on a hillside some distance away, where they planned to conduct a religious ceremony. The police had authorized the route, promising that protection could be provided, while warning that it would be impossible to prevent counter-demonstrators from throwing eggs or disrupting the march or the service. On the march to the hillside, a large number of counter-demonstrators mingled with the marchers and shouted in order to drown out the recitation of the rosary. They used the same tactic at the hillside service where around five hundred people heckled using loudspeakers, and threw eggs and clumps of grass at the physicians.

Throughout the day, riot control units had been present, but had only observed without intervening. Toward the end of the hillside ceremony, angry exchanges threatened to break out into violence. Only at that point did the riot-control units form a cordon between the opposing groups as the procession headed back to the church. Doctors for Life later filed a complaint against the police for failing to provide adequate protection. Local authorities dismissed the petition, claiming, as had earlier been warned, that full protection could not be provided against verbal abuse or throwing relatively harmless objects (although one person caught throwing eggs, which could cause physical injury, had been fined around $75). The police insisted that they had sought to avoid fueling tensions any further.

In 1982, a second demonstration was held in the cathedral square in Salzburg. Around 350 counter-demonstrators gathered. A hundred police agents formed a cordon around the demonstrators to protect them from direct attack, but tensions were heightened by the presence of a far-right political party that supported Doctors for Life. The police cleared the square so that the religious ceremony could go ahead. In further proceedings, Doctors for Life maintained that its members had received too little police protection at both demonstrations. At the European Court they claimed that the lack of police protection amounted to a violation of their freedoms of expression and association.

The European Court found that Austria had provided adequate protection, but confirmed that the duties of states signed up to the European Convention do not stop with allowing people to speak without censorship. The states have an obligation "to take reasonable and appropriate measures to enable lawful demonstrations to proceed peacefully."[43] The Court reminds us, as did Justices Black and Douglas in *Feiner*, that free speech is not a purely "negative" or "hands off" right. It requires protective conduct by the state if it is to offer safe and reliable forums for dissent. As no two political demonstrations will be identical, guidelines cannot be precisely stated, but must be provided to the extent that "[t]he participants must . . . be able to hold the demonstration without having to fear that they will be subjected to physical violence by their opponents."[44]

Despite such similarities between the American and European courts, differences across the Atlantic have also sparked debate, as illustrated by another U.S. case. In 1964 Clarence Brandenburg, a Ku Klux Klan leader, telephoned a Cincinnati television station and invited a reporter to attend a rally to be held on an Ohio farm. The reporter and a camera operator filmed the events with the cooperation of the organizers. Portions of the films were later broadcast on local and national television. One film showed twelve hooded figures, some with firearms, gathered around a large, burning cross. Both films contained invective against blacks and Jews, such as: "Personally, I believe the nigger should be returned to Africa, the Jew returned to Israel."

Brandenburg was convicted under a state criminal syndicalism statute, which prohibited advocacy of "the duty, necessity, or propriety of crime, sabotage, violence, or unlawful methods of terrorism as a means of accomplishing industrial or political reform." He was also convicted for gathering with a "society, group, or assemblage of persons formed to teach or advocate the doctrines of criminal syndicalism." Brandenburg was fined $1,000 and sentenced to a prison term of between one and ten years. But in the 1969 case of *Brandenburg v. Ohio*,[45] the U.S. Supreme Court reversed the conviction. The justices held that government may not constitutionally forbid advocacy even of the use of force, or of a violation of the law, unless such advocacy is directed to inciting or producing *imminent* lawless action, and is *likely* to incite or produce such action. As the Court explains, "The mere abstract teaching . . . of the moral propriety or even moral necessity for a resort to force and violence is not the same as preparing a group for violent action and steeling it to such action."[46] If Brandenburg had taken a step further, calling upon his mob to proceed directly to assail persons or property, then the line from speech to criminal action would have been crossed. But simply discussing repugnant ideas among themselves and posing in offensive garb with firearms, and allowing those activities to be filmed, could not constitute a crime.

With that decision, the United States became an outlier among democracies. If we examine the best-performing states in the *Democracy Index*, we find that their domestic legal codes all include bans on extreme speech, particularly when it is racist or otherwise directed against vulnerable social groups. As to non-democracies or weak democracies, clearly there are governments that simply use hate speech bans in order to crack down on perceived political enemies.[47] Just as clearly, there are regions in the world where intergroup hostilities run high, and where a government may lack the means to guarantee protections to potential victims of violence or discrimination. Since such conflict areas remain deeply embedded in local cultural histories, any one-size-fits-all rule for the globe would be naïve.

So we face a conundrum. The world's top democracies, which count among the few states that can genuinely be called human rights regimes, clearly reject viewpoint absolutism. Over the years their legal systems have steadily adopted or expanded bans on racist, sexist, homophobic, transphobic, terrorist, and other extreme speech. Those bans certainly penalize fighting words, as does U.S. law. However, they also prohibit certain forms of extreme speech uttered in the public sphere, in the form of general ideas expressed to general audiences. For example, were activities similar to those in *Brandenburg* to be discovered today in a Western European state, the state might well impose a criminal penalty, though not necessarily steep. For the most part, only for repeat or otherwise aggravated offenses do penalties start to become heavier, and such cases tend to be few. The decisive point is that most democracies wish to maintain the prerogative to impose bans on extreme speech within the public sphere, bans that U.S. law forbids under *Brandenburg*.

Such bans comply with leading human rights treaties. For example, the International Covenant on Civil and Political Rights (ICCPR) provides: "Any advocacy of national, racial or religious hatred that constitutes incitement to discrimination, hostility or violence shall be prohibited by law."[48] Similarly, the International Convention on the Elimination of All Forms of Racial Discrimination (CERD) provides that all states that are parties to the Convention:

(a) Shall declare an offence punishable by law all dissemination of ideas based on racial superiority or hatred, incitement to racial discrimination. . . .

(b) Shall declare illegal and prohibit organizations, and also organized and all other propaganda activities, which promote and incite racial discrimination, and shall recognize participation in such organizations or activities as an offence punishable by law.[49]

One reason commonly recited to justify such bans is that human rights would become self-contradictory if they were to extend so far as to include the freedom to deny openly the humanity or rights of others.[50] To be sure, in cases where extremists pass from hateful words to violent physical actions against members of vilified groups, there is greater agreement across democracies about the legitimacy of criminal sanctions. For example, although U.S. law permits hate speech of the *Brandenburg* type, it still allows states to increase penalties on hate crimes including murder, battery, vandalism, and the like, when a discriminatory motive can be shown.[51] Within top-performing democracies, advocates of extreme speech bans argue that the bans affect only small quantities of speech. Yet once ideas can legitimately be banned on grounds of expressing an unacceptable opinion, then it can be hard to find a logical stopping point. So can viewpoint absolutism still be maintained as a necessary condition for a human rights system? Or must we opt for something like "near absolutism"? If so, then how near does "near" have to be, and who should have the authority to silence whom? Line drawing between admissible and inadmissible viewpoints constantly becomes politicized, which would seem to leave the discursive principle on shaky footing.

Elsewhere I have acknowledged that hate speech attacks values of democracy, dignity, and equality, but I have cast doubt on whether bans, within strong democracies, offer either politically legitimate or pragmatically effective solutions to combating violence and discrimination against historically denigrated groups.[52] Along with others, I have argued that, particularly in an internet age, only well-organized, proactive counter-speech, promoted through early education, is likely to make any serious progress in curbing hateful speech. According to one common misperception, failing to adopt bans means that a state ends up passively accepting discrimination by sitting back and doing nothing.[53] But that view lacks any serious foundation. It is true that the strongest democracies maintain hate speech bans but, I have argued, their good human rights performance owes more to their comprehensively proactive policies, promoting pluralist values from the earliest ages through educational curricula, media campaigns, and other anti-discrimination efforts, with bans having at best little impact and more likely aggravating the problem. For example, I have argued that Germany's success in promoting Holocaust awareness has arisen not through the country's bans on Holocaust denial, but through its post-World War II educational, media, and public awareness initiatives.[54]

Viewpoint absolutism surely could be adopted by a small number of top-tier democracies. The best-performing human rights states all meet the criteria of what can be called longstanding, stable, and prosperous democracies. They are longstanding in the sense that democratic culture has largely seeped into attitudes, expectations, and practices over time, beyond the sheer dictates of an "on paper" democratic constitution. They are stable in the sense that they have had no need in recent times to undertake wide-reaching suspensions of rights on grounds of national security. And they are prosperous in the sense that they have the means to protect vulnerable groups without having to impose viewpoint-selective bans on general ideas expressed to general audiences.[55] I would maintain that viewpoint absolutism remains the appropriate benchmark.

However, realities are more complicated than benchmarks. The problems of extreme speech will remain divisive for a long time, so we need to decide whether the discursive principle must include the freedom to engage in extreme speech. After all, if the very possibility of human rights depends on the discursive principle, then the most unsatisfying result would be for all of human rights to fall hostage to this controversy. Yet on closer inspection, there is no sense in which anything I have argued in this book decisively hinges on whether one's preferred free speech model is "viewpoint absolutist," along the classical U.S. First Amendment lines, or, so to speak, "viewpoint near-absolutist," along the lines of other top-performing democracies. The freedom to engage in hate speech stands as an exceptionally controversial manifestation of viewpoint absolutism, but the more salient point is that the world's strongest democracies overwhelmingly agree in protecting free and open discussion on endless numbers of topics germane to the promotion of human rights. The top-performing democracies host criticism and protest against government, and a diversity of political viewpoints, to degrees rarely witnessed in history.

Notwithstanding differences of opinion on extreme speech, what is more important is that those democracies are set up to perform as genuine human rights states.

The twentieth-century cases I have discussed in this chapter all set forth core principles of viewpoint absolutism or near-absolutism. Yet they seem to say too little, given how twenty-first century electronic media have transformed the public sphere. Strictly speaking, for as long as social media companies are privately owned and operated, they remain free to censor as much as they like. On that traditionally contractual model, we join a social media site just as we would join a private club. We can be suspended or expelled under the terms of our contractual duties.

The problem is that the public sphere has now been taken over by these private corporations. Live street speeches and protests still take place, but the most powerful forums now exist online. Even live events have come to depend on online mobilization. The virtual public sphere is supervised by unelected corporate managers and anonymous, often transnationally outsourced employees. With whatever pragmatic justifications they may have, these corporations often fail to respond to public and user concerns, or they do so in opaque ways, and their censorship criteria seem random. Their murky policy-making prioritizes shareholder profits, not high-minded commitments to mass enlightenment. To be sure, it remains legitimate for moderators to censor online harassment targeted at identifiable individuals, under the fighting words doctrine, or for the state to intervene with penalties. Nevertheless, people have become dissatisfied across the political spectrum. Some would censor as little as possible, and would allow even postings glorifying brutality or anti-democratic violence. Others would censor far more by vigorously tackling extreme or otherwise dangerous speech, but then in ways that can become difficult to apply with any consistency, given the sheer quantities of daily postings.[56]

The banning of Donald Trump from major social media sites in January 2021[57] sent a strong symbolic message, but the long-term benefits of such a measure remain doubtful, largely because millions of like-minded people cannot so easily be silenced, both for reasons of democratic principle and monitoring pragmatics. That problem applies both to censoring an individual like Trump and to censoring an idea: there are undeniably powerful public welfare grounds for banning "deep state" theories, climate change denialism, pandemic conspiracy theories, and other dangerous opinions, yet fair and efficient monitoring becomes a formidable task when millions of people hold such views.

Overall, however, the internet has little impact on the model of human rights I have proposed in this book. Despotic states have merely drawn the internet into their sphere of repression, steadily progressing from traditional managerialism toward ever more air-tight, ever more terrifying managerialism, but not otherwise changing their managerial stances. As to democracies, some citizens would complain that their human rights have become impaired through the dissemination of extreme speech, while others would argue that their rights are damaged through online censorship of such speech, but, again, that debate reverts back to the one I have thus far been discussing. The pragmatics of handling extreme speech will continue to unfold,[58] but the dilemma of choosing between viewpoint absolutism and viewpoint near-absolutism will remain, generally with negligible consequences for citizens' pursuit of their human rights. If an otherwise strong democratic state were to start manipulating the internet so as to censor nonextreme speech in order to suppress political dissent, that would mean that the democracy was eroding, thereby jeopardizing its status as a state set up to perform human rights.

Finally, recall that I began this book noting that human rights presuppose civic equality. We are still left with the puzzle that equality would seem to claim a more foundational status than free speech. What, then, is the justification for making free speech foundational? Recall that article 2 of the Universal Declaration sets forth nondiscrimination as a condition for the enjoyment of all other rights: "Everyone is entitled to all the rights and freedoms set forth in this Declaration, without distinction of any kind, such as race, colour, sex, language, religion, political or other opinion, national or social origin, property, birth or other status." That norm has been reiterated in countless other human rights documents, and is widely recognized as international customary law.

The free speech required to found human rights certainly presupposes some level of equality, and yet the persistence of inequality raises questions about whether or when sufficient equality is present for all voices to be heard. Even in the countries with the best human rights records we find great gaps of wealth, and the wealthy can generally gain easier direct or indirect access to the public sphere. Yet that is precisely why it is free speech, and not equality, which sets the condition for human goods to become human rights. Viewpoint absolutism, or even viewpoint near-absolutism, can be established with considerable certainty. In well-performing human rights states like Norway or New Zealand, which do ban various forms of extreme speech, citizens can nevertheless remain confident about their access to public discourse in order to speak about endless problems concerning human rights.

We can identify steep inequalities in many democracies, but what counts as sufficient equality has always been controversial, and often depends on preferred economic models. If one household has $10,000 to pour into a political or public interest campaign, while another household must spend that money on care for an elderly relative, does the inequality mean that the second household has been unfairly excluded from the public sphere? Or simply placed at a tolerable disadvantage? Those critical of free speech regimes argue that power imbalances between groups make a level playing field impossible, and yet such imbalances pervade most societies. Some will respond that such an example, merely comparing two imaginary houseolds, is simplistic. It depicts inequality as random, whereas the pressing concern should be about groups that have faced entrenched inequalities over generations. Such critics argue that members of historically subordinated groups lack equally powerful voices in the public sphere. Yet those who take that position rarely pinpoint in rigorously economic terms the level of equality that would be required. If it lies only at an adequate minimum, as required by the ICESCR treaty, then considerable inequalities across groups are still permitted.

In 2015 the University of Manchester Free Speech and Secular Society invited the writer Julie Bindel to participate in a debate about conflicts between feminism and free speech. Bindel had earlier sparked anger through her refusal to equate trans women with those born as biological women. The University Student Union blocked the invitation, causing Bindel to be disinvited (or "canceled" or "no-platformed").[59] Some would call this an example of systemic imbalances in the public sphere: persons who are born biologically as women but reject equality for trans women, particularly when added to men who reject trans identities, far outnumber trans people.

The problem with that argument is not that it is wrong, but that it is too right by half. Countless social problems throughout history have entailed power imbalances—poverty, global warming, economic globalization, access to health care, political repression, corporate power, political corruption, discrimination. It is often the power imbalance that *makes* them social problems. Strictly speaking, the idea that an exponent of the more powerful position should be excluded would render it impossible to candidly discuss any of those issues. Debate would cede to recitations of one-sided doctrine.

In particular, the powerlessness of many groups is often equated with inequalities inherent with capitalism. That being the case, it would be necessary to boycott most Western economics departments daily, until their staff, even the left-leaning ones, were entirely replaced with staff who categorically oppose capitalism, and arguably any other anti-egalitarian economics, in any form. Such a campaign would actually be easier to wage, because such departments are already set up at home, so they do not depend upon the serendipity of special invitations issued to outsiders. Yet it seems that such an obvious opportunity to oppose those who promote regimes of sociopolitical power imbalances has gone entirely unnoticed, which raises serious questions about how, exactly, activists are defining their concepts of inequality and power imbalances.

Free speech does presuppose civic equality, but for purposes of setting up a human rights regime it presupposes only enough to ensure citizens' safe access to a robust sphere of public discourse. In other words, it is still free speech that remains decisive. Norway and New Zealand perform well once we assume the threshold of civic equality required for citizens to have access to public discourse. But if we were to set our threshold at perfectly equal access to public discourse, perhaps measured by equal levels of household income (or equal levels of household income after different households' particular needs were taken into account), then we would be unable to qualify even those countries as human rights regimes, and the enterprise of human rights would start to look otherworldly. Only free speech, be it through viewpoint absolutism or through viewpoint near-absolutism, can count as a comprehensive condition for the existence of human rights. Equality is to be fought for, as are all human rights, and, within a human rights regime, the only arms for such a battle are words. By contrast, there is no such thing as fighting for free speech by means of words, except insofar as free speech is already presupposed.

* * *

To sum up this chapter, drawing acceptable limits to free speech remains perennially controversial, but trying to define one open-ended principle such as "freedom" in terms of another, such as "harm," does little to solve the most controversial problems. The distinction between content-based and viewpoint-based restrictions has proven more fruitful. At least some content-based restrictions are uncontroversial, such as prohibitions on fraudulent advertising, courtroom perjury, defacing property, or individually targeted fighting words. By contrast, the problem of extreme speech will continue to be divisive, but overwhelmingly the world's top-performing democracies do not discriminate on grounds of viewpoint. Their democratic cultures are pluralist, offer wide scope for political dissent, and have created vigorous frameworks for genuine human rights systems.

7 CONCLUSION

Notions of justice are as old as humanity itself. Many ancient systems certainly urge governments to treat their people with care, and human rights present another such system. In recent years, experts have hastened to emphasize the overlaps between older belief systems and human rights. Yet, however strong those overlaps may be, some important questions have received too little attention. What do human rights do that no other system does? Many belief systems provide for human goods, but what does it mean for such goods to become the objects of human rights?

One essential element of human rights is their egalitarianism. Throughout much of human history, societies have been structured hierarchically, even if their belief systems sometimes contained egalitarian ideals. Views differ as to how much equality human rights require but, at the very least, all citizens must enjoy enough equality to be able to pursue their rights. To be sure, although ancient justice systems often presupposed hierarchical collectivities, they can certainly change to become compatible with human rights. Ancient systems have always adjusted to new circumstances, and in much of the world today egalitarian expectations are stronger than in the past. However, we cannot underestimate the demands that human rights place on other systems, insofar as human rights presuppose a safe and robust sphere of free speech, including possibilities to openly, candidly, and at times even crudely criticize governments and their officials.

Closely related to egalitarianism is the individualism of human rights. For millennia humans had been bound to collectivities based on kinship, clan, class, caste, religion, or other such affiliations. However, in Western philosophy an important change begins in the seventeenth century. Thomas Hobbes proposes a comprehensive political blueprint, in which individuals are bound to no kinship group, no clan, no class—to no authoritative entity at all, except the sovereign. For Hobbes, individuals are born with full natural rights, but then gladly sacrifice those rights to the sovereign in return for the promise of civil peace. That schema, whereby all individuals are born with full, natural rights that they then give away surely marks out a strange beginning in the march toward modern notions of human rights. However, for the first time in political philosophy, Hobbes places the individual rights holder at the foundation of politics.

Another seventeenth-century luminary, René Descartes, further defines the individual of human rights, even though he is not primarily a political philosopher. Descartes postulates human beings as able to reason independently of Church, State, and other established authorities. Certainly, since the nineteenth century, Cartesian individualism has come in for searing criticism. Writers from Hegel to Heidegger reject notions of society derived from sheer aggregates of self-sufficient, isolated, atomized individuals. Human rights have nevertheless persisted, yet we must bear in mind how disruptive their individualist and egalitarian assumptions have been from broader historical and anthropological perspectives. Although some recent writers have grounded human rights in more strongly interpersonal and communal models, those models cannot extend so far as to obliterate the individualism that protects our choices to exercise our human rights without others maintaining any veto power over those choices.

Concepts like "justice," "fairness," and other such terms are too open-ended to yield obvious interpretations. They can often be interpreted in conflicting ways. The same holds true of the concept of "rights." The fact that some eighteenth-century charters of rights remain largely intact today by no means implies that interpretations have been uniform over time. In the nineteenth century societies that had adopted such charters construed them to align with racial, gender, colonial, and other forms of discrimination. Marx rejects human rights entirely, insisting that they entrench elite interests under the guise of universally shared values. By contrast, some figures, such as Elizabeth Cady Stanton, Frederick Douglass, and Susan B. Anthony persist with existing frameworks, reinterpreting rights to show that they lack meaning unless they are understood to include racial minorities and women.

By the twentieth century, writers like Wesley Hohfled and Hans Kelsen, seeking a specifically legal concept of rights, argue that a legal right necessarily correlates to a legal duty. I refer to that relationship as the duty principle. Later writers take the next step, drawing the conclusion that human rights correlate to state duties. Indeed, the problem of vagueness within the concept of rights was never the greatest obstacle facing the emergence of an international system. The chief stumbling block was sovereigntism. For as long as a system of international law had been in existence, it had always been assumed that the way governments treated their citizens was a matter of domestic concern. The process of internationalizing human rights would have to proceed gingerly.

The primary vehicle for launching an international law of human rights, and for creating such duties, was through treaties, whereby states would be bound only insofar as they had consented. Of course, many consented more as public relations exercises than through any serious commitment to rights. Nevertheless, some of the leading treaties have achieved broad assent, and human rights have steadily moved to the center of international concern. Treaty law has increasingly been supplemented by customary human rights law, whereby states incur duties even if they had never consented to them. The complex systems of international human rights, overseen by a myriad of monitoring bodies, have created considerable redundancy, whereby many institutions perform seemingly similar tasks. However, they have also contributed to the worldwide dissemination of rights consciousness. Mass consciousness is often the most powerful channel for human rights work in a world in which other means of pursuing rights may be limited, often for reasons of sheer cost.

The Universal Declaration of Human Rights had already included a wide variety of rights, which have tended to expand as the current international systems have matured. Yet that expansion poses problems for the movement's universalist aspirations. Despite long lists of international human rights, the official policy remains that of "indivisibility," or at least "non-subordination," whereby no one right is deemed to be more important than any others. That principle would pose no problems if all rights were cost free, but the opposite is the case. Old distinctions between supposedly cost-free "negative" rights and costly "positive" rights have proved too simplistic. The more accurate view is that all rights presuppose considerable costs if they are to be reliably implemented.

Yet given that all states operate under financial constraints, non-subordination becomes financially impossible. Indeed, the opposite policy becomes compulsory: a policy of trade-offs, which we find everywhere practiced but nowhere formally acknowledged, as the myth of non-subordination continues to be upheld. Once we are in a world of necessary trade-offs, states can more easily justify neglecting some rights in order to attend to others. A monitoring body can certainly take note of that neglect, but once limited resources are assumed, as they must be, then it can do little more. In practice, a state can justify diverting resources away from humane policing in order to pour them into agricultural development, or away from safe prison conditions in order to put them into housing.

Free speech, too, can be traded off against other goods, meaning that such a system becomes indistinguishable from a managerial regime of goods. The current regimes can never become international human *rights* regimes, and were never conceived as such, despite the ubiquitous reiterations of the phrase "human rights." My objection is not of the pragmatic kind commonly heard—it is not about lack of political will or inadequate resources, although those certainly are problems. Rather the problem is conceptual. If human rights are to retain a distinct meaning, if they are not to collapse into managerial regimes of goods that render the very concept of a right superfluous, then we must identify more precisely the necessary ingredients of a human right. I take no position, then, on whether the current international systems are or are not the best possible ones under current circumstances. They may well be. My only point is that they are not human *rights* systems. The duty principle is essential, but more is required.

A right by definition entails the possibility of making a claim. It assumes at least as much free speech as the claim requires. Yet given the breadth of interests covered by human rights, and given that human rights are not always pursued through formal judicial channels, the scope of speech must necessarily be vast. Free speech within a safe and robust public sphere stands as the ultimate recourse for individuals who, rightly or wrongly, believe their rights have been violated or neglected. Only within that sphere of public discourse can state-managed human goods become objects of citizen-directed human rights. Although history has certainly known various types of regimes admitting relatively broad freedoms of speech, that has often meant that the freedom to speak today could be withdrawn or even punished tomorrow. Only in a constitutional democracy is free speech intrinsic to citizenship.

Delineating the sphere of public expression can be difficult, but some basic elements are incontestable. For example, not everything uttered in public places counts as public discourse. Insults directly targeted at identifiable individuals have long been recognized as "fighting words," which cannot in any serious sense be called part of the general ideas directed at general audiences, and can legitimately be banned. However, that does not mean that speech must be tame. Speech that does direct general ideas toward general audiences must be able to include hostility toward the government or public officials and policies. A robust public sphere certainly remains compatible with certain content-based restrictions on speech, such as bans on fraudulent advertising, courtroom perjury, or defacing of property. However, that sphere of public discourse presupposes that government may not censor ideas based solely on their viewpoints, nor may it dress up viewpoint-selective limits as content-selective ones, such as blanket "national security" or "public order" offenses.

Of course, some problems still remain, notably disagreements about how to deal with extreme speech, which the top-performing human rights regimes generally prohibit to some degree. However, that controversy, although serious, in no way undermines the central thesis that human goods become objects of human rights only insofar as citizens enjoy a safe and robust sphere of public discourse. Whether that sphere is viewpoint absolutist or viewpoint near-absolutist will remain a hard question, but must not blind us to the fact that the best human rights states, albeit near-absolutist, are also states that admit historically unprecedented levels of dissent and protest.

Only within that kind of democratic culture can a human rights system come into existence. More faltering democracies, such as the United States, India, or Brazil, have committed massive and systemic rights abuses, but for as long as those abuses can be candidly raised in the public sphere, then identifying those abuses *as* human rights abuses makes sense. By contrast, to purport to apply human rights criteria to states that, through pervasive repression of the public sphere, are not even set up to perform human rights, is to destroy the concept of human rights, confirming that genuinely citizen-directed human rights have never seriously been distinguished from purely state-monopolized, managerial regimes of human goods—which are not mere variants of human rights, but their arch-opposite. When we end up seeing two wholly contradictory conceptions as identical, then it only proves that we never had any clear idea to start with, however frequently and however confidently we were reciting it. Now is the time for human rights to be rethought. International organizations have built an impressive cathedral of human goods, but it is now time to nail a few theses about human rights to its door.

Acknowledgments

Some of the discussions in this book are adapted from "The Myth of Flexible Universality," *Oxford Journal of Legal Studies* 39, no. 3 (2019): 624–653, and from "Global Libertarianism: How Much Public Morality Does International Human Rights Law Allow?," *International Theory* (forthcoming, 2022). I would like to thank colleagues who provided feedback either on earlier drafts of the entire text or on papers that became sections of it, including John Adenitire, Ian Cram, Helena Drakakis, John Drakakis, Kristian Skagen Ekeli, Adrian Howe, Rosa Freedman, David McGrogan, Les Moran, Jo Murkens, Richard Nobles, Ioanna Tourkochoriti, Steven Wheatley, William Wilson, and Mark Wolfgram. I would also add my appreciation for the thoughtful recommendations offered by each of the MIT Press's anonymous reviewers.

I am grateful for opportunities I have had to present ideas set forth in this book at several events, including a presentation at the colloquium "Just Memories: Remembrance and Restoration in the Aftermath of Political Violence," chaired by Jeremy Sarkin and hosted online by the legal publishing house Intersentia, December 2020; a presentation at the conference "Consistency in Human Rights," chaired by Noele Crossley at the Oxford Department of International Development (ODID), Oxford University, December 2019; a guest lecture chaired by Fabrizio Sciacca at the Dipartimento di Scienze Politiche e Sociali, Università degli Studi di Catania, Italy, November 2019; a presentation at the conference "Multi-disciplinary Approaches to Contemporary Issues in Religion and Society," chaired by

Sylvie Bacquet at the University of Westminster, October 2019; a presentation at the conference "Muslim Minorities and Human Rights," Centre for Arab Progress, University of London, September 2019; a special guest lecture chaired by Torkel Brekke at Civita-akademiet, Oslo, Norway, May 2019; participation in the conference on "Heritage and Change," Lund, Sweden, May 2019, collaboratively hosted by The Wallenberg Foundation (Sweden), Carlsberg Foundation (Denmark), Compagnia di San Paolo (Italy), Volkswagen Foundation (Germany), and Riksbankens Jubileumsfond (Sweden); a presentation at the conference "Democracy as Interpretation," hosted by Emanuela Fronza and Paolo Caroli, Università di Bologna, Italy, March 2019; a presentation at the "Conference on Systems Theory and Human Rights," hosted by Steven Wheatley, Centre for Law & Society, Lancaster University, October 2018; a presentation at the conference "Time, Memory and Criminal Law," hosted by Emanuela Fronza, Università di Bologna, Italy, May 2018; a guest lecture organized by Jorge Núñez and hosted by Gavin Phillipson at the Juris North Working Paper Series, Durham Law School, Durham University, UK, March 2017; a guest lecture organized by Matteo Bonotti at the Political Theory Research Seminar, Political Theory Research Unit, Cardiff University, UK, February 2017; and a guest lecture hosted by Rob Jago at the Department of Law and Criminology, Royal Holloway, University of London, December 2016. For my participation at both of the aforementioned Bologna conferences, I am grateful for generous funding provided by the European Union HERA (Humanities in the European Research Area) program, in my capacity as Project Leader for the four-nation MELA consortium (Memory Laws in European and Comparative Perspective, 2016–2019).

Finally, heartfelt thanks are due for the support and patience of my literary agent, Jaime Marshall, as well as Julia Collins for her careful proofreading, along with my editors Gita Devi Manaktala and Kathleen Caruso at the MIT Press.

Appendix: Universal Declaration of Human Rights

PREAMBLE

Whereas recognition of the inherent dignity and of the equal and inalienable rights of all members of the human family is the foundation of freedom, justice and peace in the world,

Whereas disregard and contempt for human rights have resulted in barbarous acts which have outraged the conscience of mankind, and the advent of a world in which human beings shall enjoy freedom of speech and belief and freedom from fear and want has been proclaimed as the highest aspiration of the common people,

Whereas it is essential, if man is not to be compelled to have recourse, as a last resort, to rebellion against tyranny and oppression, that human rights should be protected by the rule of law,

Whereas it is essential to promote the development of friendly relations between nations,

Whereas the peoples of the United Nations have in the Charter reaffirmed their faith in fundamental human rights, in the dignity and worth of the human person and in the equal rights of men and women and have determined to promote social progress and better standards of life in larger freedom,

Whereas Member States have pledged themselves to achieve, in co-operation with the United Nations, the promotion of universal respect for and observance of human rights and fundamental freedoms,

Whereas a common understanding of these rights and freedoms is of the greatest importance for the full realization of this pledge,

Now, Therefore THE GENERAL ASSEMBLY proclaims THIS UNIVERSAL DECLARATION OF HUMAN RIGHTS as a common standard of achievement for all peoples and all nations, to the end that every individual and every organ of society, keeping this Declaration constantly in mind, shall strive by teaching and education to promote respect for these rights and freedoms and by progressive measures, national and international, to secure their universal and effective recognition and observance, both among the peoples of Member States themselves and among the peoples of territories under their jurisdiction.

ARTICLE 1

All human beings are born free and equal in dignity and rights. They are endowed with reason and conscience and should act towards one another in a spirit of brotherhood.

ARTICLE 2

Everyone is entitled to all the rights and freedoms set forth in this Declaration, without distinction of any kind, such as race, colour, sex, language, religion, political or other opinion, national or social origin, property, birth or other status. Furthermore, no distinction shall be made on the basis of the political, jurisdictional or international status of the country or territory to which a person belongs, whether it be independent, trust, non-self-governing or under any other limitation of sovereignty.

ARTICLE 3

Everyone has the right to life, liberty and security of person.

ARTICLE 4

No one shall be held in slavery or servitude; slavery and the slave trade shall be prohibited in all their forms.

ARTICLE 5

No one shall be subjected to torture or to cruel, inhuman or degrading treatment or punishment.

ARTICLE 6

Everyone has the right to recognition everywhere as a person before the law.

ARTICLE 7

All are equal before the law and are entitled without any discrimination to equal protection of the law. All are entitled to equal protection against any discrimination in violation of this Declaration and against any incitement to such discrimination.

ARTICLE 8

Everyone has the right to an effective remedy by the competent national tribunals for acts violating the fundamental rights granted him by the constitution or by law.

ARTICLE 9

No one shall be subjected to arbitrary arrest, detention or exile.

ARTICLE 10

Everyone is entitled in full equality to a fair and public hearing by an independent and impartial tribunal, in the determination of his rights and obligations and of any criminal charge against him.

ARTICLE 11

(1) Everyone charged with a penal offence has the right to be presumed innocent until proved guilty according to law in a public trial at which he has had all the guarantees necessary for his defence.

(2) No one shall be held guilty of any penal offence on account of any act or omission which did not constitute a penal offence, under national or international law, at the time when it was committed. Nor shall a heavier penalty be imposed than the one that was applicable at the time the penal offence was committed.

ARTICLE 12

No one shall be subjected to arbitrary interference with his privacy, family, home or correspondence, nor to attacks upon his honour and reputation. Everyone has the right to the protection of the law against such interference or attacks.

ARTICLE 13

(1) Everyone has the right to freedom of movement and residence within the borders of each state.

(2) Everyone has the right to leave any country, including his own, and to return to his country.

ARTICLE 14

(1) Everyone has the right to seek and to enjoy in other countries asylum from persecution.

(2) This right may not be invoked in the case of prosecutions genuinely arising from non-political crimes or from acts contrary to the purposes and principles of the United Nations.

ARTICLE 15

(1) Everyone has the right to a nationality.

(2) No one shall be arbitrarily deprived of his nationality nor denied the right to change his nationality.

ARTICLE 16

(1) Men and women of full age, without any limitation due to race, nationality or religion, have the right to marry and to found a family. They are entitled to equal rights as to marriage, during marriage and at its dissolution.

(2) Marriage shall be entered into only with the free and full consent of the intending spouses.

(3) The family is the natural and fundamental group unit of society and is entitled to protection by society and the State.

ARTICLE 17

(1) Everyone has the right to own property alone as well as in association with others.

(2) No one shall be arbitrarily deprived of his property.

ARTICLE 18

Everyone has the right to freedom of thought, conscience and religion; this right includes freedom to change his religion or belief, and freedom, either alone or in community with others and in public or private, to manifest his religion or belief in teaching, practice, worship and observance.

ARTICLE 19

Everyone has the right to freedom of opinion and expression; this right includes freedom to hold opinions without interference and to seek, receive and impart information and ideas through any media and regardless of frontiers.

ARTICLE 20

(1) Everyone has the right to freedom of peaceful assembly and association.

(2) No one may be compelled to belong to an association.

ARTICLE 21

(1) Everyone has the right to take part in the government of his country, directly or through freely chosen representatives.

(2) Everyone has the right of equal access to public service in his country.

(3) The will of the people shall be the basis of the authority of government; this will shall be expressed in periodic and genuine elections which shall be by universal and equal suffrage and shall be held by secret vote or by equivalent free voting procedures.

ARTICLE 22

Everyone, as a member of society, has the right to social security and is entitled to realization, through national effort and international co-operation and in accordance with the organization and resources of each State, of the economic, social and cultural rights indispensable for his dignity and the free development of his personality.

ARTICLE 23

(1) Everyone has the right to work, to free choice of employment, to just and favourable conditions of work and to protection against unemployment.

(2) Everyone, without any discrimination, has the right to equal pay for equal work.

(3) Everyone who works has the right to just and favourable remuneration ensuring for himself and his family an existence worthy of human dignity, and supplemented, if necessary, by other means of social protection.

(4) Everyone has the right to form and to join trade unions for the protection of his interests.

ARTICLE 24

Everyone has the right to rest and leisure, including reasonable limitation of working hours and periodic holidays with pay.

ARTICLE 25

(1) Everyone has the right to a standard of living adequate for the health and well-being of himself and of his family, including food, clothing, housing and medical care and necessary social services, and the right to security in the event of unemployment, sickness, disability, widowhood, old age or other lack of livelihood in circumstances beyond his control.

(2) Motherhood and childhood are entitled to special care and assistance. All children, whether born in or out of wedlock, shall enjoy the same social protection.

ARTICLE 26

(1) Everyone has the right to education. Education shall be free, at least in the elementary and fundamental stages. Elementary education shall be compulsory. Technical and professional education shall be made generally available and higher education shall be equally accessible to all on the basis of merit.

(2) Education shall be directed to the full development of the human personality and to the strengthening of respect for human rights and fundamental freedoms. It shall promote understanding, tolerance and friendship among all nations, racial or religious groups, and shall further the activities of the United Nations for the maintenance of peace.

(3) Parents have a prior right to choose the kind of education that shall be given to their children.

ARTICLE 27

(1) Everyone has the right freely to participate in the cultural life of the community, to enjoy the arts and to share in scientific advancement and its benefits.

(2) Everyone has the right to the protection of the moral and material interests resulting from any scientific, literary or artistic production of which he is the author.

ARTICLE 28

Everyone is entitled to a social and international order in which the rights and freedoms set forth in this Declaration can be fully realized.

ARTICLE 29

(1) Everyone has duties to the community in which alone the free and full development of his personality is possible.

(2) In the exercise of his rights and freedoms, everyone shall be subject only to such limitations as are determined by law solely for the purpose of securing due recognition and respect for the rights and freedoms of others and of meeting the just requirements of morality, public order and the general welfare in a democratic society.

(3) These rights and freedoms may in no case be exercised contrary to the purposes and principles of the United Nations.

ARTICLE 30

Nothing in this Declaration may be interpreted as implying for any State, group or person any right to engage in any activity or to perform any act aimed at the destruction of any of the rights and freedoms set forth herein.

Notes

EPIGRAPH

1. "Le vrai but de la politique n'est pas d'administrer le moins mal possible le bien commun" (Viansson-Ponté, "Quand la France," 1). Translations from Western European languages in this book are the author's, unless otherwise indicated.

CHAPTER 1

1. UN-HRC, Communication No. 2054/2011, paras. 2.1–2.6.

2. UN-HRC, Communication No. 2001/2010, paras. 2.1–2.5.

3. UN-HRC, Communication No. 1773/2008, paras. 2.1–2.14. Transliterations of proper names tend to vary, but the UN report translates Казулін as "Kozulin," and Аляксандр is often translated as "Alyaksandr" or "Alyaksander."

4. The committee found that Kyrgyzstan had violated Ernazarov's right to life, as well as his rights not to be subjected to torture or to cruel, inhuman, or degrading treatment or punishment. Denmark had discriminated against Q on grounds of disability, violating his right to equal protection under the law. Belarus had violated Kazulin's rights to fair conditions of arrest, trial, and detention. In 2019, a Kyrgyz court ordered the country's Ministry of Finance to pay compensation to Ernazarov's family. In view of Q's anonymity, no further information on his case is available. See "Ministry of Finance of Kyrgyzstan" (2019). Kazulin had been released from prison in 2008. See "Belarus Dissident Leaves Prison" (2008). As of this writing, the Danish Institute for Human Rights confirms that Q's identity has remained anonymous (electronic message dated Apr. 3, 2020, on file with author).

5. See generally, e.g., Confucius, *Analects*. The *Analects* were not directly authored by Confucius, but instead record his views according to disciples. Cf. Hsi and Lü, *Reflections*, 183–259. On Confucianism and human rights, see, e.g., de Bary and Weiming, *Confucianism and Human Rights*; Kim, "Confucianism, Moral Equality"; Sang-Jin, "Confucianism and Human Rights"; Sim, "A Confucian Approach"; Tiwald, "Confucianism and Human Rights."

6.	*Politics* 1287ª30–32, in Aristotle, *Complete Works*, 2042–2043.

7.	Qur'an 16:90. On Islam and human rights, see, e.g., An-Na'im, "Universality and Human Rights"; An-Na'im, "Islam and Human Rights"; An-Na'im, "Compatibility Dialectic"; An-Na'im, "Complementary, Not Competing"; Baderin, *International Human Rights*; Baderin, "Human Rights and Islamic Law"; Bassiouni, *Menschenrechte*; Emon, Ellis, and Glahn, "From 'Common Ground'"; Saeed, *Human Rights and Islam*.

8.	Aquinas, *Summa Theologica*, ST I-II q.96 a. 1, 791. On Christianity and human rights, see, e.g., Moyn, *Christian Human Rights*; Tierney, *Idea of Natural Rights*.

9.	On Buddhism and human rights, see, e.g., Loy, "A Different 'Enlightened' Jurisprudence?"; Nehring, "Human Rights"; Schmidt-Leukel, "Buddhism." On Hinduism and human rights, see, e.g., Sharma, *Hinduism and Human Rights*; Desai, "Duties and Rights in Hinduism"; Tarasco, "Hinduism and Human Rights." On Jainism and human rights, see, e.g., Shah, "Human Rights." On Taoism and human rights, see, e.g., Palmer, "Daoism and Human Rights."

10.	See chapter 4, 55–56.

11.	For a classic exposition see Lauterpacht, *International Bill*. For recent histories see, e.g., Jensen, *Making of International Human Rights*; Moyn, *Last Utopia*.

12.	For drafting histories, see, e.g., Glendon, *World Made New*; Morsink, *Universal Declaration of Human Rights*.

13.	For one of the classic polemics insisting on the hollowness of the concept of human rights, see Bentham, "Anarchical Fallacies." For a contemporary study of the malleability of concepts and norms in international law, see, e.g. Koskenniemi, *Apology to Utopia*.

14.	See chapter 3, 43.

15.	UDHR art. 4.

16.	Confucius, *Analects* 14.22, 234. The inserted explanatory text is the translator's.

17.	*Matthew* 5:39, in Coogan, *New Oxford Annotated Bible*, 1754. The same observation holds true for unwritten legal systems. For example, if law for a given people is delivered case by case by councils of elders, then vagueness can arise about what one may and may not do in future situations that are similar but not identical.

18.	UDHR, preamb. para. 8.

19.	In addition to the Bill of Rights, further constitutional rights have been recognized through amendment or judicial interpretation.

20.	See chapter 4, 64.

21.	Henkin, *Age of Rights*, xvii.

22.	For criticisms of contemporary human rights systems from various perspectives, see, e.g., Brown, "*The Most*"; Douzinas, *End of Human Rights*; Douzinas, *Human Rights and Empire*;

Hopgood, *Endtimes of Human Rights*; Marks, "Human Rights and Root Causes"; Mutua, *Human Rights*; Posner, *Twilight of Human Rights Law*.

23. For discussions about technocracy and managerialism in international law and in human rights, see, e.g., Kennedy, *World of Struggle*; McGrogan, *Critical Theory and Human Rights*.

24. See chapter 4, 67–68.

25. Studies have been undertaken in various countries to examine public support toward human rights, often with encouraging results. For present purposes, however, such publications yield too-limited information, since none of them measures human rights according to the conception that I propose in this book, so the dangers of both interviewers and interviewees confusing rights with goods becomes patent.

26. Cf. Beitz, *Idea of Human Rights*, 106 (describing human rights in terms of sociolinguistic practice).

27. See chapter 5, 93–94.

CHAPTER 2

1. I use the word "differentialism" rather than "discrimination" in order to avoid the appearance of passing anachronistic value judgments on earlier societies, and to avoid debates about whether or when unequal treatment would have been justified. In addition, I qualify these two models as "civic" because not all differentialist or egalitarian relationships are of concern to human rights. For example, most of us would want someone without medical training to be treated unequally to a qualified physician for purposes of performing heart surgery. Only insofar as we are civic actors, and potentially political actors, do differentialist or egalitarian relationships become decisive for human rights. Moreover, for me to use the term "egalitarianism" without the qualification "civic" would raise questions about the degree of equality that human rights demand. However, having stated those caveats, I shall in practice usually drop the qualifier "civic" in order to unburden the prose, on the understanding that I am always assuming it when I discuss differentialism or egalitarianism.

2. Ephesians 6:5, in Coogan, *New Oxford Annotated Bible*, 2059.

3. Ephesians 5:22, in Coogan, 2058.

4. Confucius, *Analects* 17.25, 295.

5. Confucius, 295. Many Maoists originally criticized Confucianism for its classism and sexism, but in recent years leaders have bolstered Chinese nationalism by rehabilitating that tradition. For example, the Confucian Temple compound in the Dongcheng district of Beijing currently includes an exhibit displaying that tradition in a positive light.

6. Commentary by Wing-Tsit Chan, in Hsi and Lu, *Reflections* VI: 13, 177 n. 21.

7. Hsi and Lu, *Reflections* VI: 13, 177.

8. Commentary by Wing-Tsit Chan, in Hsi and Lu, *Reflections* VI: 13, 177 n. 21.

9. See, e.g., Becker, "Politics, Differences and Economic Rights"; Minow, "Rights for the Next Generation; Minow, "Interpreting Rights"; Nedelsky, *Relations of Freedom*.

10. I correlate differentialism to *hierarchical* collectivism since there have also been collectivist regimes claiming to be egalitarian. For example, in the twentieth century, socialist states collectivized industry and agriculture. Leaving aside questions as to how egalitarian they really were, they certainly did recreate collectivities to which the individual owed ongoing duties. To denote that kind of system, we would have to substitute the term "individualism" in figure 2.1 with some phrase such as "egalitarian collectivism."

11. See, e.g., Vanderlinden, *Anthropologie juridique*.

12. Confucius, *Analects* 12.11, 186.

13. Confucius, 8.14, 124.

14. These matters are examined throughout the *Analects*, and then more systematically throughout Hsi and Lu, *Reflections* VI–IX, 183–237.

15. See generally, e.g., Hsi and Lu, *Reflections* VI, 171–182.

16. Shakespeare offers a vivid example of the self-evidence of different justice for different classes in earlier times. In *Henry VI, Part Two* commoners are sentenced to grueling deaths for treason, while the aristocrat who had incited them, being "more nobly born" (Shakespeare, *Henry VI, Part Two* 2.3.9, 167), is sentenced to three days of public penance followed by banishment.

17. See chapter 5, 84–90.

18. See chapter 6, 121–124.

19. Confucius, *Analects* 12.1, 179.

20. See generally, e.g., Confucius, X, 146–160.

21. Confucius, 15.39, 266.

22. See, e.g., Gadamer, *Wahrheit und Methode*, 312–346.

23. See, e.g., Gao and Yan, "The Source"; Nuyen, "Confucianism." Despite Confucianism's powerful influence over thousands of years, it should not be assumed that ordinary Chinese would call themselves "Confucian," or expressly designate Confucianism as central to their indentities in the ways we commonly witness within the Abrahamic traditions. As Sungmoon Kim observes, "East Asians are saturated with Confucian habits and mores [but] are not Confucians in a philosophically monist and culturally monolithic sense." Kim, "Confucianism, Moral Equality," 151–152.

24. *Meno* 70a in Plato, *Complete Works*, 871.

25. *Meno* 71d–72a in Plato, 872.

26. *Meno* 81a in Plato, 880 (emphasis added).

27. In the *Symposium*, Plato has Socrates discussing essential pillars of Platonic philosophy, which Socrates claims to have learned from Diotima of Mantinea, "a woman who was wise about many things." *Symposium* 201d, in Plato, *Complete Works*, 484. Cf., e.g., Annas, "Plato's *Republic* and Feminism"; Fine, "Inquiry in the *Meno*."

28. On the status of slavery and equality in Plato's thought, see, e.g., Vlastos, *Platonic Studies*, 147–203.

29. See, e.g., *Émile* I, in Rousseau, *Oeuvres Complètes* (vol. 4), 250.

30. *Republic* 2.374e–4.434c, 5.474b–7.541b, in Plato, *Complete Works*, 1013–1066, 1101–1155.

31. *Politics* 1.1.1152^{a}15–16, 2.2.1261^{b}4–5, 4.17.1288^{a}15, 6.2.1317^{b}1–16 in Aristotle, *Complete Works*, 1986, 2001, 2044, 2091.

32. *Politics* 1.4.1253^{b}31–32, in Aristotle, 1989.

33. *Politics* 1.12.1260^{a}12–13, in Aristotle, 1999.

34. *Politics* 1.12.1260^{a}13–14 in Aristotle, 1999.

35. See, e.g., Homiak, "Feminism and Aristotle's Rational Ideal."

36. See Menke and Pollmann, *Philosophie der Menschenrechte*, 99 (observing the difficulty of expressly speaking out against human rights today).

37. Cf., e.g., Fisher, Horwitz, and Reed, *American Legal Realism*; Leiter, *Naturalizing Jurisprudence*.

38. Cf. Hart, "Positivism," 607. Formalism and realism may themselves be subject to disputed interpretations, and they are joined by other styles of analysis. On responses to Hart, see, e.g., Fuller, "Positivism and Fidelity to Law," 663; Schauer, "Formalism," 526.

39. See chapter 6, 121–124.

40. On criteria for assessing states, see chapter 5, 93–94.

41. The word "irrespective" in tables 2.1 and 2.2 does not preclude causation between formal and real law, but suggests only that causation between them is not strictly necessary. Certainly, real law often arises as a result of formal law, but does not always or necessarily arise in that way.

CHAPTER 3

1. See, e.g., Jensen, *Making of International Human Rights*.

2. Cf., e.g., Menke and Pollmann, *Philosophie der Menschenrechte*, 98.

3. See, e.g., UDCD, preamb. paras. 1–2; art. 4. Cf. critically, e.g., Manent, *La loi naturelle*, 2–8 (linking that contradiction to inconsistent uses of the concept of universality).

4. That transformation has remained among the prime topics of modern sociology since its grounding in the nineteenth century. See, e.g., Tönnies, *Gemeinschaft und Gesellschaft*.

5. See, e.g., UN-CEDW and UN-CRC, "Joint General Recommendation No. 31" (condemning practices undertaken in the name of cultural and community tradition, such as discrimination against women generally, and oppression of girls in particular through female genital mutilation [FGM], child or forced marriage, polygamy, and honor crimes).

6. The ITP was adopted by the General Conference of the International Labour Organization in 1989.

7. ITP art. 1(1)(b).

8. ITP art. 3(1).

9. Cf. Heinze, review of *La question des peuples sutochtones*, by I. Schulte-Tenckhoff.

10. See, e.g., Bruun-Solbakk and Stubberud, "Sápmi Pride."

11. See, e.g., UN-CEDW and UN-CRC, "Joint General Recommendation No. 31."

12. For an overview, see, e.g., Davies, *Europe*, 213–468.

13. See, e.g., Davies, *Europe*, 469–575; Edney, *Cartography*. On the modern legal concept of statehood, see, e.g., Crawford, *Creation of States*.

14. Translated from Hobbes's Latin autobiography, "Tomae Hobbes Malmesburiensis," lxxxvi.

15. See, e.g., Martinich, *Two Gods of Leviathan*, 362–368.

16. Hobbes, *Leviathan*, chs. 13–14, 100–116.

17. Hobbes, ch. 14, 106.

18. Hobbes, ch. 13, 102.

19. Hobbes, ch. 13, 104.

20. Hobbes, ch. 13, 103.

21. Hobbes, ch. 18, 141–150. Hobbes suggests that a right to life is in some form retained (Hobbes, ch. 14, 108), but its force remains doubtful, given that the absolute sovereign is by definition unanswerable to any individual or institution.

22. See, e.g., Hobbes, ch. 21, 171–182. In that respect, Hobbes actually makes no break from much standard medieval and Rennaissance thought, as had been embodied in the popular "mirror for magistrates" tradition. See, e.g., Erasmus, *Education of a Christian Prince*.

23. Cf., e.g., Strauss, "Hobbes' politische Wissenschaft," 150; Menke, *Kritik der Rechte*, 22–29.

24. On human rights as a legitimating criterion for the contemporary state, see, e.g., Menke and Pollmann, *Philosophie der Menschenrechte*, 103.

25. Hobbes, *Leviathan*, ch. 6, 43.

26. See, e.g., Lloyd, *Bloomsbury Companion to Hobbes*; Martinich and Hoekstra, *Oxford Handbook of Hobbes*; Sorell, *Cambridge Companion to Hobbes*.

27. See, e.g., Waldron, "Hobbes and the Principle of Publicity."

28. See, e.g., Schmitt, *Der Leviathan* (approvingly); Agamben, *Homo Sacer* (admonishingly); Agamben, *State of Exception* (admonishingly).

29. Martel, *Subverting the Leviathan*. That kind of "subversive" reading certainly has distinguished predecessors. For example, Rousseau read Machiavelli the same way. *Du Contrat Social* III:6, in Rousseau, *Oeuvres Complètes* (vol. 3), 409.

30. Cf. Rawls's notion of a "decent hierarchical society." Rawls, *Law of Peoples*, 71–78.

31. See, e.g., UN-HRC (USA), Concluding observations; UN-CEDW (India), Concluding observations; UN-CRC (Brazil), Concluding observations.

32. But see Descartes, *Les passions de l'âme*, 691–802. See also, e.g., Guenancia, *Descartes et l'ordre politique*; Kolesnik-Antoine, *Descartes*.

33. Descartes, *Discours de la méthode*, 128, 130–131, and passim.

34. Descartes, *Méditations* [Première], 267–273.

35. Descartes, *Méditations* [Deuxième], 274–283.

36. Mill, *On Liberty*, ch. 2, 20–61.

37. See Kant, *Grundlegung*; Kant, *Kritik*; Kant, *Die Metaphysik der Sitten*.

38. See, e.g., Heinze, "Democracy, Ontology."

39. See, e.g., Heinze, "The Myth of Flexible Universality."

40. Locke, *Second Treatise*, chs. 11–13 (paras. 134–158), 66–81.

41. DI preamble.

42. Locke, *Second Treatise*, chs. 11–12 (paras. 134–148), 66–74.

43. In international law a more specialized vocabulary has also arisen, including concepts such as "peremptory norms," "*jus cogens*," and "obligations *erga omnes*." See, e.g., ILC, Second Report; Orakhelashvili, *Peremptory Norms*.

44. Cf., e.g., UN-HRC, General Comment 24; UN-HRC, General Comment 29; UN-HRC, General Comment 31.

45. See, e.g., Marx, "Zur Judenfrage"; Marx, "Kritik des Gothaer Programms." In those works, however, Marx by no means disputes the values underlying a number of human rights (see, e.g., Heinze, "Karl Marx's Theory"), a problem that has prompted longstanding debates about the compatability of Marxism with human rights. See, e.g., O'Byrne, "Marxism and Human Rights."

46. Locke, *Second Treatise*, ch. 5 (paras. 41–44), 22–24. For a critical assessment, see, e.g., Uzgalis, "John Locke, Racism."

47. Some readers have challenged that link between Locke and individualism, emphasizing instead his, and indeed early liberalism's, Christian roots. Locke seems to have feared that by grounding ethics ultimately in the individual this would mean that the individual "could have no law but his own will, no end but himself. He would be a god to himself, and the

satisfaction of his own will the sole measure and end of all his actions." See, e.g., an unpublished note from ca. 1693 (Bodleian MS Locke c. 28, fo. 141). See also Waldron, *God, Locke*. But that interpretation has also attracted criticism. See, e.g., Andrew, "Reviewed Work"; Nuovo, review of *God, Locke and Equality*, by Jeremy Waldron; Stolzenberg and Yaffe, "Waldron's Locke." Similarly, John Dunn has challenged dominant secular-liberal and Marxist readings of Locke, also stressing his theological underpinnings. See Dunn, *Political Thought of John Locke*. Be that as it may, today there is no serious way to construe Lockean higher-order rights except as fundamentally individualist.

48. See, e.g., Habermas, *Theorie*.

49. DDHC, art. 1.

50. See, e.g., Hegel, *Phänomenologie des Geistes*, 430–440.

51. See, e.g., Hegel, *Phänomenologie des Geistes*, 423–430, 440–452.

52. See, e.g., Hegel, *Grundlinien* §§142–181, §§257–320, and §§ 291–306, 397–489.

53. See, e.g., Marx, *Zur Kritik*; Popper, *Open Society*.

54. See, e.g., Beiser, *Hegel*, 224–258.

55. Kant, *Zum ewigen Frieden*; Kant, *Metaphysik der Sitten*.

56. On different types of democracies and the concept of a top-performing democracy, see chapter 5, 93–94.

57. Marx, "Zur Judenfrage."

58. See, e.g., Brown, "*The Most*"; Douzinas, *End of Human Rights*; Douzinas, *Human Rights and Empire*; Marks, "Human Rights and Root Causes"; Mutua, *Human Rights*.

59. Heidegger, *Über den Humanismus*, 12–16, 51. Heidegger's anti-Semitism and allegiance to Nazism, shared by some of those other figures of the time, have prompted extensive debate about his critiques of humanism and modernity, not unlike critiques of other anti-Semitic or pro-fascist modernists. See, e.g., Homolka and Heidegger, *Heidegger und der Antisemitismus*; Trawny, *Heidegger und der Mythos*.

60. See Heidegger, *Über den Humanismus*; Heidegger, "Zeit des Weltbildes." But compare Sartre's strong individualism. Sartre, *L'Être et le Néant*, 487–692; Sartre, *L'Existentialisme est un humanisme*. See also Merleau-Ponty, *Phénoménologie*, 345–468, 496–520.

61. Heinze, "Democracy, Ontology."

62. American Anthropological Association, "Statement," 542.

63. In his attempt to discern what is distinctive about humans, Aristotle follows the same path. What he ends up finding is our capacity for *logos*, which in ancient Greek denotes not only reason but also speech. *Logos* is private and contemplative, but also communicative, carrying more the sense of openly shared ideas. For Aristotle, what makes humans distinctive is not only our rational but also our communicative capacities. *Nicomachean Ethics* 1.7.1097^{b}32–1098^{a}8, in Aristotle, *Complete Works*, 1735.

64. American Anthropological Association, "Statement," 542. For a more recent statement, see American Anthropological Association, "Declaration." But see, critically, Heinze, "The Myth of Flexible Universality," 651n99.

65. See critically, e.g., Manent, *La loi naturelle*, 3; Menke and Pollmann, *Philosophie der Menschenrechte*, 76–77.

66. See, e.g., Hitler, *Mein Kampf*, 346, 421, 479 (condemning norms of human equality as a corrupted "judification" of Western civilization).

67. See, e.g., Russian Constitution 1918, article 1; USSR Constitution 1936, chapter 10.

68. Cf., e.g., UN-CEDW and UN-CRC, "Joint General Recommendation No. 31."

69. See, e.g., Kim, "Confucianism, Moral Equality," 149–152. Cf. An-Na'im, "Compatibility Dialectic"; Baderin, "Human Rights and Islamic Law"; Saeed, *Human Rights and Islam*, 1–7.

70. An-Na'im, "Islam and Human Rights," 95.

71. An-Na'im, 95–96.

72. An-Na'im, 96. An-Na'im's reference to the traditional *theology* of the major *religions*, being more suited to the Abrahamic monotheisms, is slightly awkward, but his basic point is sound.

73. UNESCO, "Human Rights," 1 (original emphasis).

74. UNESCO, "Human Rights," 1 (emphasis added).

75. Dred Scott v. Sandford, 60 U.S. (19 How.) 393 (1857).

76. Bradwell v. State of Illinois, 83 U.S. (16 Wall.) 130 (1873).

77. Plessy v. Ferguson, 163 U.S. 537 (1896). See also, e.g., Douglas, *Jim Crow Moves North*; Foner, *Second Founding*; Higginbotham, *Ghosts of Jim Crow*; Klarman, *From Jim Crow*.

78. Lochner v. New York, 198 U.S. 45 (1905).

79. 198 U.S. 45 at 53.

80. 198 U.S. 45 at 52–53. See also, e.g., Balkin, "'Wrong the Day." The case continues to spark debate. See, e.g., Bernstein, *Rehabilitating Lochner*; Kens, "History and Implications of *Lochner v. New York*." For example, Bernstein argues that the state legislation was supported in part to curb competition from bakers employing immigrant labor. Bernstein, *Rehabilitating Lochner*, 23.

81. Walker, "Frederick Douglass."

82. See, e.g., Jones, "The US Suffragette Movement."

83. See, e.g., Douglass, "What to the Slave Is the Fourth of July."

84. Anthony, "On Women's Right."

85. See, e.g., Douzinas, *End of Human Rights*; Douzinas, *Human Rights and Empire*.

86. See, e.g., Wolton, *Le Négationnisme*.

CHAPTER 4

1. Hohfeld, "Some Fundamental Legal Conceptions," 30 (original emphasis), citing *Lonas v. State*, 3 Heisk. (Tennessee), 287 (1871), 306–307. Cf. Kelsen, *Reine Rechtslehre*, 131.

2. See "Wesley Newcomb Hohfeld."

3. Hohfeld, "Some Fundamental Legal Conceptions," 30.

4. See, e.g., Prott, *Politics of Self-Determination*.

5. Olechowski, *Hans Kelsen*.

6. See, e.g., Austin, *Province of Jurisprudence Determined*. First promoted by English utilitarians, legal positivism gained further momentum from post-Enlightenment campaigns to systematize legal norms and procedures. For example, on the continent Napoleonic-type codes started to shape an orderly framework out of previously fragmented bodies of law. See, e.g., Goyard-Fabre, *Les fondements*, 109–162.

7. Hohfeld, "Some Fundamental Legal Conceptions," 30–31, 43. Kelsen fully explains the idea only in his book's second edition (Kelsen, *Reine Rechtslehre*, 131), whereas Hohfeld had worked it out by 1913.

8. See, e.g., Donnelly and Whelan, *International Human Rights*, 49–69; Kühnhardt, *Die Universalität*, 174–278.

9. Cf., e.g., Donnelly and Whelan, *International Human Rights*, 27, 33–35.

10. In contemporary international human rights law, entities other than states can also incur duties to respect human rights. See, e.g., Bantekas and Oette, *International Human Rights Law*, 761–804. In other words, X holds a human right only if the state owes a corresponding legal duty to X, although other entities may also owe that duty to X. In principle, the model I am developing would apply equally to nonstate governing authorities, such as provisional and transitional bodies. Yet in practice, such bodies often oversee turbulent regions, where political disputes and everyday crises can make it difficult to implement human rights. Other nonstate actors include private individuals and companies. Ideally, if a private actor were to violate my human rights, then it would be the duty of the state to provide redress, usually through ordinary criminal, tort, contract, or other such areas of law. Failure to do so would constitute a violation on the part of the state. Of course, corrupt or weak states often fail to do so, but then that is no different from failing to respond to state violations. That principle of "third-party applicability of human rights" continues to develop. Today, moreover, multinational corporations can be more difficult for individual states to regulate, or individual states may lack incentives to police them for economic reasons. See, e.g., EC, "Tackling Illegal Content." I shall briefly revisit that problem in chapter 6, 120–121, but my focus in this book is on states.

11. See, e.g., Heller, *Sovereignty*. For critical discussions of the history of international law, see, e.g., Fassbender and Peters, *Oxford Handbook*.

12. See, e.g., Orakhelashvili, *Akehurst's Modern Introduction*, 6–8.

13. For comprehensive annual reports, see, e.g., See Economist Intelligence Unit, *Democracy Index* (annual); Reporters Without Borders, *World Press Freedom Index* (annual); Transparency International, *Corruption Perceptions Index* (annual). For further ongoing updates, see also Amnesty International, Human Rights Watch, Article 19, Index on Censorship, and Freedom House.

14. See, e.g., Freedman, *United Nations Human Rights Council.*

15. Opinions vary about the political and social factors that propelled international recognition of human rights after World War II. See, e.g., Jensen, *Making of International Human Rights*; Moyn, *Last Utopia*, 120–175.

16. See, e.g., Aust, *Modern Treaty Law*; Gardiner, *Treaty Interpretation.*

17. See, e.g., Cranston, *What Are Human Rights?*, 65–69. For a more recent exposition of that view, see, e.g., Rhodes, *Debasement of Human Rights.* John Rawls, too, endorses a narrow list, limited to rights deemed essential to maintaining international order. Rawls, *Law of Peoples*, 78–81.

18. See, e.g., Schrijver, "Fifty Years."

19. See, e.g., Bantekas and Oette, *International Human Rights Law*, 192–338; de Schutter, *International Human Rights Law*, 935–1040; Rehman, *International Human Rights Law*, 84–351. The African Union formerly went by the name of the Organization of African States.

20. A controversial exception is the African Charter on Human and Peoples' Rights, which reintroduces notions of individual duties to family and community, and emphasizes collective rights that some have viewed with skepticism. ACHPR arts. 19–26, 27(1). The African Union formerly went by the name of the Organization of African States.

21. CRC arts. 14(1), 15(1). As with most other CRC rights, arts. 14(1) and 15(1) are neither unlimited nor preclusive of the involvement of parents or guardians. See CRC arts. 14(2), 15(2), 15(3). We also witness expansion of human rights since 1948 in sources other than multilateral treaties. For example, according to a UN General Assembly Resolution from 1990, identifying a problem scarcely discussed in 1948, "all individuals are entitled to live in an environment adequate for their health and wellbeing." NEHE, preamb. para. 1.

22. See, e.g., Cole, "Effects of Human Rights"; Koob, Jørgensen, and Sano, "Human Rights and Economic Growth."

23. See, e.g., Kinzelbach, "China's Rise."

24. See this chapter, 63–64.

25. See PPCG.

26. According to Article III: "The following acts shall be punishable: (a) Genocide; (b) Conspiracy to commit genocide; (c) Direct and public incitement to commit genocide; (d) Attempt to commit genocide; (e) Complicity in genocide." For further background and

commentary, see, e.g., Gaeta, *UN Genocode Convention*; Irvin-Erickson, *Raphael Lemkin and the Concept of Genocide*.

27. See, e.g., ILC, Second Report, para. 46, 25–26.

28. Posner, *Twilight of Human Rights Law*, 7.

29. Shelton, review of *Twilight*, by Eric Posner, 229.

30. Shelton, 229.

31. For a comprehensive defense of the current international regimes, see Sikkink, *Evidence for Hope*.

32. See this chapter, note 17. See also, e.g., Berlin, *Four Essays*, 122–131. By the late nineteenth century, technological advances such as wiretapping prompted concerns about new forms of government intrusion into the personal sphere. Louis Brandeis advocated a right to privacy, a right that had not appeared in any general terms in the Enlightenment-era charters of individual rights, calling it a "right to be left alone." Olmstead v. United States, 277 U.S. 438, 478 (1928) (Brandeis, J., dissenting). See also Warren and Brandeis, "Right to Privacy." That idea of a "right to be left alone" has since been used to depict more broadly the notion of a "negative" or "hands off" right to individual freedom.

33. See, e.g., Applebaum, *Red Famine*; Dikötter, Mao's Great Famine; Dolot, Execution by Hunger.

34. See, e.g., Hutton, Haller, and Bartram, "Global Cost-Benefit."

35. See, e.g, Feygin, "Chernobyl Shows How."

36. See, e.g., AccessNow, *Fighting Misinformation*; Cooper, "Chinese State Censorship."

37. See, e.g., Donnelly and Whelan, *International Human Rights*, 32.

38. ICESCR art. 2(1).

39. For discussions of solidarity rights, see, e.g., Alston, "Third Generation"; Donnelly, "In Search of the Unicorn"; Padilla, "Intergenerational Equity." To some extent solidarity rights overlap with individual rights, despite their collective character. For example, the European Court of Human Rights has interpreted the individual's rights to life and to peaceful enjoyment of home and property as meaning that member states have an obligation to protect citizens from dangerous or polluting substances. See, e.g., Pedersen, "European Court"; San José, *Environmental Protection*. In that sense, an individual right can be construed to encompass a collectivized interest. Even so, some would argue that individual rights cannot fully satisfy the demands of solidarity rights, and, in any event, problems like climate change and global pandemics render purely national solutions futile. On that view, the imperatives of collective self-preservation may certainly invite us to reap the benefits of global trade, but must also impose the burdens of collective and fairly apportioned prevention and redress.

40. See, e.g., UN-ESC (Norway), Concluding observations; Blom, *Armoede in Nederland*.

41. VDPA, para. 5. For further discussion, see, e.g., Donnelly and Whelan, *International Human Rights*, 73–87; Gilabert, "Importance of Linkage"; Nickel, "Rethinking Indivisibility"; Nickel, "Indivisibility and Linkage Arguments"; Whelan, *Indivisible Human Rights*.

42. Nickel, "Rethinking Indivisibility," 985.

43. UN-ESC (Mali) para. 12, 3.

CHAPTER 5

1. See, e.g., UN-ESC (Norway), Concluding observations.

2. Hohfeld, "Some Fundamental Legal Conceptions," 32. Many writers have since employed the concept of a "claim right" to capture the specifically legal meaning of a "right." See, e.g., Finnis, *Natural Law*, 199.

3. Kelsen, *Reine Rechtslehre*, 132.

4. Feinberg, "Nature and Value," 150.

5. Feinberg, 150 (original emphasis).

6. Feinberg, 150 (the parenthetical insertion of "performative" is Feinberg's). Cf. Menke, *Kritik der Rechte*, 56 (arguing that a legal right is "a claim to have claims realized").

7. The objection is quoted from comments submitted anonymously in response to a draft version of this chapter (on file with author).

8. Cf., e.g., Wittgenstein, *Philosophische Untersuchungen*, 239–257.

9. In a U.S. Supreme Court case upholding public flag burning as legally protected speech, even the dissenting justices did not question the communicative character of the protest. See Texas v. Johnson, 491 U.S. 397 (1989).

10. Cf., e.g., Ekeli, "Democratic Legitimacy"; Ekeli, "Toleration, Respect for Persons."

11. Kant, "Über den Gemeinspruch," 161. See also Foucault's analysis of *parrhēsia* in the pre-human rights society of ancient Athens. Foucault, *Le gouvernement*.

12. For the sake of precision, I use the phrase "within a safe and robust sphere of public expression" as opposed to "through a human right of free speech" to avoid the appearance of a vicious circle. After all, one might wonder: how can there already be a human right to free speech *if* the free speech right is a precondition for human rights to exist? But there is no vicious circle. I am positing free speech as a necessary condition for the existence of rights because I am not deriving other rights from the free speech right. Nor does free speech in the public sphere exhaust the scope of the free speech right. Some speech would rarely if ever enter an individual's pursuit of human rights, but still merits protection alongside other human rights. The free speech I am advocating as a necessary condition does not erase the more conventional free speech rights under UDHR, ICCPR, ECHR, etc. See Heinze, *Hate Speech*, 84–86. I would also add that debates have long taken place about how to describe what a right protects. Some writers advocate an "interest theory," which states that

the function of rights is to protect certain interests of rights-holders. Others embrace a "will theory," whereby the individual gains active control over the duty-holder by being able to lay claims. Within the context of higher-order rights held against the state, both theories presuppose that a *claim to* a right can be laid, but neither has generally been correlated to any compulsory sphere of public discourse that would guarantee a wide scope for *claiming that*. As to human rights, then, the interest theory and the will theory both presuppose the duty principle, but partisans of both theories have overlooked the discursive principle.

13. Sen, "Freedom Favors Development," 26.

14. See, e.g., Langlois, "Human Rights without Democracy"; McGinnis, "Democracy."

15. An argument might be made that both free expression and free association would be necessary, since *claiming that* achieves nothing without an audience. But that is one reason why I speak not of free speech in the abstract, but specifically of opportunities to speak in an open, public sphere in order to speak to others. After all, freedom of association protects relationships, such as purely private contacts, which may or may not form part of the open pursuit of rights. By presupposing access to the public sphere, the discursive principle entails sufficient access to live or online audiences for open scrutiny of government to be full and effective. As to freedom of association in contexts unrelated to the open pursuit of rights, that still remains a right in itself alongside all other rights, but not foundational in the sense that free speech must be. I am grateful to Stephan Parmentier for raising this concern.

16. While singling out free speech as a necessary condition *for* human rights, I assume no further stance on questions of indivisibility or nonsubordination within that system after it has been established. The discursive principle remains compulsory regardless of one's choice of corpus. By extension, I assume no further hierarchy of rights, as some have proposed. See, e.g., Quintavalla and Heine, "Priorities and Human Rights."

17. Finnis, *Natural Law*, 199–205. Finnis excludes free expression from what he calls the "basic forms of human good" (e.g., 59–80). On a generous reading, the best one can surmise is that free expression in his schema serves a purely instrumental role, valuable only insofar as it promotes one or more of the goods he does include. The most obvious of those would be knowledge (e.g., 59–80), which, however, implies nothing sufficiently determinate about the necessary discursive conditions either for the pursuit of knowledge, or for the pursuit of any other goods *as* the objects of rights. Finnis tacitly rejects Aristotle's concept of reason (*logos*), by which speech (*logos*) constitutes reason as inherent to the human, and does not boil down only to knowledge (*epistēmē*). See *Nicomachean Ethics* 1.7.1097^{b}32–1098^{a}8, in Aristotle, *Complete Works*, 1735.

18. Like most observers broadly writing within the classically liberal vein, Griffin certainly accords a high status to free expression, but not a foundational status. See, e.g., Griffin, *On Human Rights*, 159, 193.

19. Donnelly and Whelan, *International Human Rights*, 26.

20. Nickel, *Making Sense.*

21. See Beitz, *Idea of Human Rights,* 102–106 (comparing this method with other methods).

22. Cf. Kelsen, *Vom Wesen,* 8–9.

23. Franck, "The Emerging Right." See also Steiner, "Political Participation."

24. See, e.g., Dworkin, "Foreword"; Habermas, *Theorie*; Heinze, *Hate Speech,* 43–55, 94–99; Post, *Constitutional Domains*; Post, "Hate Speech"; and Post, "Participatory Democracy"; Weinstein, "Hate Speech Bans." That view has certainly been challenged, indeed with considerable vigor, by Jeremy Waldron. See, e.g., Waldron, "Hate Speech and Political Legitimacy"; Waldron, "Conditions of Legitimacy." However, Waldron fails to provide an adequate account of political legitimacy. See, e.g., Heinze, "Taking Legitimacy Seriously"; Weinstein, "Hate Speech Bans and Political Legitimacy." On divergent views about how free speech constitutes democracy, see, e.g., Tourkochoriti, *Freedom of Expression.* One objection to my view might evoke the prospect of an "epistemocracy," whereby the privilege to vote would be subject to some prior state examination of civic knowledge. Such a society would not be democratic in any current sense, but, the argument runs, free speech could be constitutive of it, that is, more than just another right. The idea is that even persons barred from voting could still enjoy fully-fledged free speech prerogatives. Yet it is precisely that qualification that undoes the suggestion that such a regime would be sufficiently constituted by free speech. Free speech within public discourse must amount to more than just the possibility of lower-class citizens pleading to be heard by the upper class. Free speech constitutes democracy because it constitutes democratic citizenship, which must include constitutionally guaranteed prerogatives for citizens to participate on a civically equal basis in processes of effective change. Many thanks to Kristian Skagen Ekeli for provocative discussions on this and related points.

25. See, e.g., Dalton, Shin, and Jou, "Popular Conceptions."

26. Notwithstanding the *Republic*'s notoriously censorious regime, in *Crito* Plato repeatedly emphasizes the constitutive nature of free speech within democracy. See, e.g., Heinze, "The Constitution of the Constitution." Cf. Foucault, *Le gouvernement.* But then how are we to explain Socrates' trial and death sentence? All three charges against Socrates involved speech crimes: corrupting the youth, denying Athenian gods, and seeking to introduce new goods. *Apology* 24b, in Plato, *Complete Works,* 23. None of those charges had a serious basis or precedent in Athenian law. The prosecution is widely understood today as revenge for Socrates having encouraged the youth, particularly of the upper classes, to challenge democratic norms, which some citizens saw as contributing to the Spartan victory in the Peloponnesian war, which devastated Athens. However, many others opposed the trial and sentence, and the jury probably failed to reflect a representative demographic. See, e.g., Brickhouse and Smith, *Plato and the Trial,* 85–97.

27. See, e.g., UN-HRC (Nigeria), paras. 19–20; UN-HRC (Tunisia), para. 19; UN-HRC (Uzbekistan), para. 10. On the necessary inherence of LGBTQ+ rights in previous human rights law dating back to the Universal Declaration, see, e.g., Heinze, *Sexual Orientation.*

On LGBTQ+ rights as a bellwether of individual freedom, see, e.g., Heinze, "Sexual Orientation and International Law"; Heinze, "Global Libertarianism."

28. See chapter 4, note 13. Studies placing greater stress on social and economic progress do not purport to focus specifically on democratic culture or institutions, but offer useful comparators. See, e.g., Social Progress Imperative, *Social Progress Index* (annual).

29. See, e.g, Human Rights Watch, "Russia." See generally sources cited in chapter 4, note 13.

30. Hannum, review of *Twilight*, by Eric Posner.

31. Posner, *Twilight of Human Rights Law*, 144–145 (emphasis added). Cf. Shelton, review of *Twilight*, by Eric Posner, 228.

32. Brown, "*The Most*," 457.

33. Brown, 457 (emphasis added).

34. See, e.g., Blom, *Armoede in Nederland*.

CHAPTER 6

1. Reporters Without Borders, *World Press Freedom Index*. Some might argue that all those people whose free speech rights have been violated need simply sue their local authorities in order to invoke their First Amendment rights, but matters are not so simple. For example, in cases of street protest, evidence that a protester acted peacefully may be lacking or may be flatly denied by arresting officers, who are often favored by courts. Once again the lesson is clear: rights genuinely exist only in practice, and not merely on paper, even when that paper issues from a body like the U.S. Supreme Court.

2. See, e.g., Heinze, *Hate Speech*, 40–43.

3. DDHC art 4.

4. Mill, *On Liberty*, ch. 1, 14.

5. See, e.g., Heinze, "Victimless Crimes."

6. See, e.g., Hare and Weinstein, *Extreme Speech*.

7. See, e.g., Cohen-Almagor, "J. S. Mill's Boundaries"; Ward and Mcglyn, "Would John Stuart Mill."

8. Unsurprisingly, detailed arguments have been made both favoring and opposing bans on grounds of classical liberal principles. See, e.g., Heinze, *Hate Speech*, 59–66, 88–99. Mill makes other classically liberal arguments—for example, about the enrichment of knowledge and debate through diverse views—but few writers today argue that sheer insults seriously advance those values.

9. See e,g., UN-HRC, Communication No. 1932/2010.

10. See, e.g., Heinze, *Hate Speech*, 19–22; Weinstein, "An Overview," 82–83, 86–87, 91.

11. See, e.g., Heinze, "Viewpoint Absolutism"; Heinze, *Hate Speech*, 77, 81, 82, 95; Heinze, "Taking Legitimacy Seriously."

12. My thanks to an anonymous reviewer who posed this hypothetical.

13. See, e.g., Sim, "The Singapore Chill."

14. See, e.g., New York Times Co. v. Sullivan, 376 U.S. 254 (1964); Gertz v. Robert Welch, Inc., 418 U.S. 323 (1974); Dun & Bradstreet, Inc. v. Greenmoss Builders, Inc., 472 U.S. 749 (1985).

15. The term largely translates Jürgen Habermas's concept of *Öffentlichkeit* first introduced to a wide readership in 1962. See Habermas, *Strukturwandel der Öffentlichkeit*. See also, e.g., Habermas, *Theorie*; Post, *Constitutional Domains*.

16. State v. Chaplinsky, 91 N.H. 310, 313 (1941) (emphasis added).

17. 91 N.H. at 312.

18. 91 N.H. at 312.

19. 91 N.H. at 320.

20. Chaplinsky v. New Hampshire, 315 U.S. 568, 573 (1942).

21. See, e.g., Holder v. Humanitarian Law Project, 561 U.S. 1, 40–62 (2010) (Breyer, J., dissenting).

22. See, e.g., Roth v. United States, 354 U.S. 476, 482 (1957).

23. See, e.g., Abrams v. United States, 250 U.S. 616, 624 (1919) (Holmes, J., dissenting); Gitlow v. New York, 268 U.S. 652, 673 (1925) (Holmes, J., dissenting, joined by Brandeis, J., dissenting); Whitney v. California, 274 U.S. 357, 372 (1927) (Brandeis, J., concurring).

24. Brandenburg v. Ohio, 395 U.S. 444 (1969); Matal v. Tam, 582 U.S. ____; 137 S. Ct. 1744 (2017).

25. Note also that even a fully fledged public forum entails no absolute freedom insofar as legitimate restrictions may be imposed for purposes of avoiding obstruction of people's free movement, avoiding excessive late-night noise in residential areas, and so forth. On these types of "time, manner, and place" restrictions, and on different types of public or "quasi-public" forums for free speech, see, e.g., Nowak and Rotunda, *Constitutional Law*, 1447–1475.

26. Feiner v. New York, 240 U.S. 315 (1951).

27. 240 U.S. at 321–322 (Black, J., dissenting).

28. 240 U.S. at 325.

29. UN-HRC, Communication No. 1773/2008, para 2.10.

30. Feiner v. New York, 240 U.S. at 325–326.

31. 240 U.S. at 326–327 (Black, J., dissenting) (emphasis added).

32. 240 U.S. at 331 (Douglas, J., dissenting).

33. 240 U.S. at 331 (Douglas, J., dissenting).

34. ICCPR art. 4; cf. ECHR art. 15. Under ICCPR art. 4(2) and ECHR art. 15(2), no derogation is permitted for certain rights, such as protections from torture or cruel, inhuman or degrading treatment. See, e.g., UN-HRC, General Comment 29.

35. Cohen v. California, 405 U.S. 15 (1971).

36. 405 U.S. at 20. Citing precedent, the Supreme Court also noted that the sheer presence of the word "Fuck" did not suffice to make the phrase subject to obscenity law.

37. 405 U.S. at 27 (Blackmun, J., dissenting).

38. "Putin Denounces Opponents."

39. 405 U.S. at 25. Cf. Heinze, Hate Speech, 162–165.

40. 405 U.S. at 25–26. Cf. Heinze, "Taking Legitimacy Seriously."

41. See, e.g., Stewart, "'We Are Committing Educational Malpractice.'"

42. See generally, e.g., Belavusau and Gliszczyńska-Grabias, Law and Memory.

43. Plattform "Ärtze für das Leben" v. Austria, judgment of June 21, 1988, Eur. Ct. H. R. Ser. A, No. 139, para. 34.

44. Eur. Ct. H. R. Ser. A, No. 139, at para. 32.

45. Brandenburg v. Ohio, 395 U.S. 444 (1969). Cf. Abrams v. U.S., 250 U.S. 616, 624 (Holmes, J., dissenting); Gitlow v. New York, 268 U.S. 652, 672 (1925) (Holmes, J., dissenting); Whitney v. California, 274 U.S. 357, 372 (1927) (Brandeis, J., dissenting); Dennis v. U.S., 341 U.S. 494, 579 (1951) (Black, J., dissenting) and at 581 (Douglas, J., dissenting); Beauharnais v. Illinois, 343 U.S. 250, 267 (1952) (Black, J., dissenting), at 277 (Reed, J., dissenting), at 284 (Douglas, J., dissenting), and at 287 (Jackson, J., dissenting).

46. 395 U.S. at 443–444.

47. See, e.g., Berwick and Kinosian, "Venezuela."

48. ICCPR, article 20(2).

49. ICERD, art. 4.

50. For these and related arguments, see, e.g., Delgado and Stefancic, Must We Defend Nazis?; Delgado and Stefancic, Understanding Words That Wound; Heyman, "Hate Speech"; Waldron, The Harm in Hate Speech; Langton, "Speech Acts"; Matsuda et al., Words That Wound.

51. See Wisconsin v. Mitchell, 508 U.S. 476 (1993).

52. Heinze, Hate Speech. See also, e.g., Dworkin, "Foreword"; Fronza, Memory and Punishment; Post, Constitutional Domains; Strossen, HATE; Weinstein, "Hate Speech Bans."

53. Heinze, Hate Speech, 111–112 (criticizing Waldron).

54. Heinze, 111–116, 129–137. For a defence of the dominant German position, see, e.g., Thiel, *Wehrhafte Demokratie*. For both supportive and critical arguments, see Leggewie and Meier, *Verbot der NPD*.

55. Heinze, 69–78.

56. For further analysis, see, e.g., Block and Riesewieck, *Cleaners*; Denardis, *Internet in Everything*; Kaye, *Speech Police*.

57. Denham, "These Are the Platforms."

58. For an example of a regional response to extreme speech hosted by private social media companies, see EC, "Tackling Illegal Content."

59. "'Transphobe' Julie Bindel."

Works Cited

PRIMARY INSTRUMENTS

ACHPR [African Charter on Human and Peoples' Rights]. June 27, 1981. OAU Doc. CAB/LEG/67/3 rev. 5, 21 I.L.M. 58 (1982), entered into force Oct. 21, 1986.

CEDAW [Convention on the Elimination of all Forms of Discrimination Against Women]. Dec. 21, 1979, 1249 U.N.T.S. 13 (entered into force, Sept. 3, 1981).

CRC [Convention on the Rights of the Child]. Nov. 20, 1989. 1577 U.N.T.S. 3, entered into force Sept. 2, 1990.

DDHC [*Déclaration des Droits de l'Homme et du Citoyen*] (1789). French National Assembly, Conseil constitutionnel. https://www.conseil-constitutionnel.fr/le-bloc-de-constitutionnalite/declaration-des-droits-de-l-homme-et-du-citoyen-de-1789 (accessed June 1, 2021). Official translation of the *Conseil Constitutionnel.* https://www.conseil-constitutionnel.fr/en/declaration-of-human-and-civic-rights-of-26-august-1789 (accessed June 1, 2021).

DI [Declaration of Independence]. (United States, 1776).

ECHR [European Convention for the Protection of Human Rights and Fundamental Freedoms] (as amended by Protocols Nos. 11 and 14 and supplemented by Protocols Nos. 1, 4, 6, 7, 12, 13 and 16). Nov. 4, 1950. ETS 5.

ICCPR [International Covenant on Civil and Political Rights]. Dec. 19, 1966. 999 U.N.T.S. 171 (entered into force Mar. 23, 1976).

ICERD [International Convention on the Elimination of All Forms of Racial Discrimination]. Dec. 21, 1965. 660 U.N.T.S. 195 (entered into force Apr. 1, 1969).

ICESCR [International Covenant on Economic, Social and Cultural Rights]. Dec. 16, 1966. 993 U.N.T.S. 3 (entered into force Jan. 3, 1976).

ITP [Convention concerning Indigenous and Tribal Peoples in Independent Countries] (ILO No. 169). 72 ILO Official Bull. 59 (entered into force Sept. 5, 1991).

NEHE [The Need to Ensure a Healthy Environment for the Well-Being of Individuals]. UN G.A. Res. 45/94, U.N. GAOR, 45th Sess., Supp. No. 49A, at 178. UN Doc. A/45/40 (1990).

PPCG [Convention on the Prevention and Punishment of the Crime of Genocide (Genocide Convention)]. Dec. 9, 1948. 78 U.N.T.S. 277 (entered into force Jan. 12, 1951).

Russian Constitution 1918 [Constitution (Basic Law) of the Russian Socialist Federated Soviet Republic] (1918).

UDCD [Universal Declaration on Cultural Diversity], adopted by the General Conference of the United Nations Educational, Scientific and Cultural Organization, Nov. 2, 2001.

UDHR [Universal Declaration of Human Rights], G.A. res. 217A (III), UN Doc A/810 at 71 (1948).

USSR Constitution 1936. [Constitution (Fundamental law) of the Union of Soviet Socialist Republics] (1936).

VCLT [Vienna Convention on the Law of Treaties]. May 23, 1969, 1155 U.N.T.S. 331 (entered into force Jan. 27, 1980).

VDPA [Vienna Declaration and Programme of Action], adopted by the World Conference on Human Rights in Vienna (1993).

CASES

Abrams v. United States, 250 U.S. 616 (1919).

Beauharnais v. Illinois, 343 U.S. 250 (1952).

Bradwell v. State of Illinois, 83 U.S. (16 Wall.) 130 (1873).

Brandenburg v. Ohio, 395 U.S. 444 (1969).

Chaplinsky (State v.) 91 N.H. 310, 313 (1941) [New Hampshire].

Chaplinsky v. New Hampshire, 315 U.S. 568 (1942).

Cohen v. California, 403 U.S. 15 (1971).

Dennis v. United States, 341 U.S. 494 (1951).

Dred Scott v. Sandford, 60 U.S. (19 How.) 393 (1857).

Feiner v. New York, 240 U.S. 315 (1951).

Gitlow v. New York, 268 U.S. 652, 673 (1925).

Humanitarian Law Project, 561 U.S. 1 (2010).

Lochner v. New York, 198 U.S. 45 (1905).

Lonas v. State, 3 Heisk., 287 (1871) (Tennessee).

Matal v. Tam, 582 U.S. ____; 137 S. Ct. 1744 (2017).

Olmstead v. United States, 277 U.S. 438 (1928).

Plattform "Ärtze für das Leben" v. Austria, judgment of June 21, 1988, Eur. Ct. H. R. Ser. A, No. 139.

Plessy v. Ferguson, 163 U.S. 537 (1896).

Roth v. United States, 354 U.S. 476, 482 (1957).

Whitney v. California, 274 U.S. 357 (1927).

Wisconsin v. Mitchell, 508 U.S. 476 (1993).

OFFICIAL REPORTS

EC [European Commission]. "Tackling Illegal Content Online: Towards an Enhanced Responsibility of Online Platforms." Communication of Sept. 28, 2017, 555 (final).

ILC [International Law Commission]. Second Report on *jus cogens* (Dire Tladi, Special Rapporteur). UN Doc. A/CN.4/706 (2017).UN-CEDW (India) [United Nations Committee on the Elimination of Discrimination against Women]. Concluding observations on the combined fourth and fifth periodic reports of India, July 24, 2014. UN Doc. CEDAW/C/IND/CO/4–5.

UN-CEDW and UN-CRC [United Nations Committee on the Elimination of Discrimination against Women and United Nations Committee on the Rights of the Child]. "Joint General Recommendation No. 31 of the Committee on the Elimination of Discrimination against Women / General Comment No. 18 of the Committee on the Rights of the Child," Nov. 14, 2014. UN Doc. CEDAW/C/GC/31-CRC/C/GC/18.

UN-CRC (Brazil) [United Nations Committee on the Rights of the Child]. Concluding observations on the combined second to fourth periodic reports of Brazil, Oct. 30, 2015. UN Doc. CRC/C/BRA/CO/2–4.

UN-ESC (Mali) [United Nations Committee on Economic, Social and Cultural Rights]. Concluding observations on the initial report of Mali, report of Nov. 6, 2018. UN Doc. E/C.12/MLI/CO/1.

UN-ESC (Norway) [United Nations Committee on Economic, Social and Cultural Rights]. Concluding observations on the sixth periodic report of Norway, Apr. 2, 2020.

UNESCO [United Nations Educational, Scientific and Cultral Organization]. "Human Rights." UNESCO/PHS (rev.), July 25, 1948.

UN-HRC [United Nations Human Rights Committee]. Communication No. 1773/2008. UN Doc. CCPR/C/112/D/1773/2008 (2014), Olga Kazulina v. Belarus.

UN-HRC [United Nations Human Rights Committee]. Communication No. 1932/2010. Nov. 19, 2012. UN Doc. CCPR/C/106/D/1932/2010, Fedotova v. Russian Federation.

UN-HRC [United Nations Human Rights Committee]. Communication No. 2001/2010. UN Doc. CCPR/C/113/D/2001/2010 (2015), Q v. Denmark.

UN-HRC [United Nations Human Rights Committee]. Communication No. 2054/2011. UN Doc. CCPR/C/113/D/2054/2011 (2015), Mamatkarim Ernazarov v. Kyrgyzstan.

UN-HRC (Nigeria) [United Nations Human Rights Committee]. Concluding observations on Nigeria in the absence of its second periodic report. UN Doc. CCPR/C/NGA/CO/2, report of Aug. 29, 2019.

UN-HRC (Tunisia) [United Nations Human Rights Committee]. Concluding observations on the sixth periodic report of Tunisia, UN Doc. CCPR/C/TUN/CO/6, report of Apr. 24, 2020.

UN-HRC (USA) [United Nations Human Rights Committee]. "Concluding observations on the fourth periodic report of the United States of America." Apr. 23, 2014. UN Doc. CCPR/C/USA/CO/4.

UN-HRC (Uzbekistan) [United Nations Human Rights Committee]. Concluding observations on the fifth periodic report of Uzbekistan, May 1, 2020. UN Doc. CCPR/C/UZB/CO/5.

UN-HRC [Human Rights Committee]. General Comment 24 (52). General comment on issues relating to reservations made upon ratification or accession to the Covenant or the Optional Protocols thereto, or in relation to declarations under article 41 of the Covenant. UN Doc. CCPR/C/21/Rev.1/Add.6 (1994).

UN-HRC [Human Rights Committee]. General Comment 29, States of Emergency (article 4). UN Doc. CCPR/C/21/Rev.1/Add.11 (2001).

UN-HRC [Human Rights Committee]. General Comment 31, Nature of the General Legal Obligation on States Parties to the Covenant. UN Doc. CCPR/C/21/Rev.1/Add.13 (2004).

OTHER SOURCES

AccessNow. *Fighting Misinformation and Defending Free Expression during Covid-19: Recommendations for States.* April 2020. https://www.accessnow.org/cms/assets/uploads/2020/04/Fighting-misinformation-and-defending-free-expression-during-COVID-19-recommendations-for-states-1.pdf (accessed June 1, 2021).

Agamben, Giorgio. *Homo Sacer: Sovereign Power and Bare Life.* Translated by Daniel Heller-Roazen. Stanford, CA: Stanford University Press, 1998.

Agamben, Giorgio. *State of Exception.* Translated by Kevin Attell. Chicago: University of Chicago Press, 2005.

Alston, Philip. "A Third Generation of Solidarity Rights: Progressive Development or Obfuscation of International Human Rights Law." *Netherlands International Law Review* 29 (1982): 307–322.

American Anthropological Association (Executive Board). "Declaration on Anthropology and Human Rights Committee for Human Rights American Anthropological Association," adopted by AAA membership June 1999. https://www.americananthro.org/ConnectWithAAA/Content.aspx?ItemNumber=1880 (accessed June 1, 2021).

American Anthropological Association (Executive Board). "Statement on Human Rights." *American Anthropologist (New Series)* 49, no. 4 (1947): 539–543.

Amnesty International. https://www.amnesty.org/en/ (accessed June 1, 2021).

Andrew, Edward. "Reviewed Work: God, Locke and Equality: Christian Foundations of Locke's Political Thought by Jeremy Waldron." *Journal of British Studies* 44, no. 2 (2005): 370–372.

An-Na'im, Abdullahi. "The Compatibility Dialectic: Mediating the Legitimate Co-existence of Islamic Law and State Law." *Modern Law Review* 73 (2010): 1–29.

An-Na'im, Abdullahi. "Complementary, Not Competing, Claims of Law and Religion: An Islamic Perspective." *Pepperdine Law Review* 39 (2013): 1231–1256.

An-Na'im, Abdullahi. "Islam and Human Rights: Beyond the Universality Debate." *American Society of International Law Proceedings* 94 (2000): 95–101.

An-Na'im, Abdullahi. "Universality and Human Rights: An Islamic Perspective." In *Japan and International Law*, edited by Nisuke Ando, 311–325. London: Kluwer, 1999.

Annas, Julia. "Plato's *Republic* and Feminism." In *Plato 2: Ethics, Politics, Religion and the Soul*, edited by Gail Fine, 265–279. Oxford: Oxford University Press, 1999.

Annenberg Public Policy Center of the University of Pennsylvania. "Americans Are Poorly Informed About Basic Constitutional Provisions." Report of Sept. 12, 2017. https://www.annen bergpublicpolicycenter.org/americans-are-poorly-informed-about-basic-constitutional-provi sions/ (accessed June 1, 2021).

Anthony, Susan B. "On Women's Right to Vote" (1872). *The History Place*. https://www.history place.com/speeches/anthony.htm (accessed June 1, 2021).

Applebaum, Anne. *Red Famine: Stalin's War on Ukraine*. New York: Penguin, 2017.

Aquinas, Thomas. *Summa Theologica*. Translated by Fathers of the English Dominican Province. New York: Random House, 2000 [1911–1925].

Aristotle. *The Complete Works of Aristotle: The Revised Oxford Translations*. Vols. 1 and 2, edited by J. Barnes. Princeton: Princeton University Press, 1984.

Article 19. https://www.article19.org/ (accessed June 1, 2021).

Aust, Anthony. *Modern Treaty Law and Practice*. 3rd ed. Cambridge: Cambridge University Press, 2014.

Austin, John. *The Province of Jurisprudence Determined*. Indianapolis: Hackett, 1998 [1832].

Baderin, Mashood A. "Human Rights and Islamic Law: The Myth of Discord." *European Human Rights Law Review* 2 (2005): 165–185.

Baderin, Mashood A. *International Human Rights and Islamic Law*. Oxford: Oxford University Press, 2005.

Balkin, Jack M. "'Wrong the Day It Was Decided': *Lochner* and Constitutional Historicism." *Boston University Law Review* 85 (2005): 677–725.

Bantekas, Ilias, and Lutz Oette. *International Human Rights Law and Practice*. 2nd ed. Cambridge: Cambridge University Press, 2016.

Bassiouni, Mahmoud. *Menschenrechte zwischen Universalität und islamischer Legitimität.* Frankfurt a.M.: Suhrkamp, 2014.

Becker, Mary. "Politics, Differences and Economic Rights." *University of Chicago Legal Forum* 1989, no. 1: 169–190.

Beiser, Frederick. *Hegel.* London: Routledge, 2005.

Beitz, Charles. *The Idea of Human Rights.* Oxford: Oxford University Press, 2011.

"Belarus Dissident Leaves Prison." BBC News, Aug. 16, 2008. http://news.bbc.co.uk/1/hi/world /europe/7565695.stm (accessed June 1, 2021).

Belavusau, Uladzislau, and Aleksandra Gliszczyńska-Grabias, eds. *Law and Memory: Towards Legal Governance of History.* Cambridge: Cambridge University Press, 2017.

Bentham, Jeremy. "Anarchical Fallacies." In *On Utilitarianism and Government*, 383–459. London: Wordsworth, 2001 [1796].

Berwick, Angus, and Sarah Kinosian. "Venezuela Wields a Powerful 'Hate' Law to Silence Maduro's Remaining Foes." *Reuters*, Dec. 14, 2020. https://www.reuters.com/investigates/special-report/venezuela-politics-hatelaw/ (accessed June 1, 2021).

Berlin, Isaiah. *Four Essays on Liberty.* Oxford: Oxford University Press, 1969.

Bernstein, David E. *Rehabilitating Lochner: Defending Individual Rights against Progressive Reform.* Chicago: University of Chicago Press, 2011.

Block, Hans, and Moritz Riesewieck, dir. *The Cleaners.* Nov. 12, 2018. New York: Motto Pictures.

Blom, Robert Jan. *Armoede in Nederland.* Soesterberg, NL: Aspekt B.V, 2019.

Bowen, Catherine Drinker. *Miracle at Philadelphia: The Story of the Constitutional Convention.* Boston: Back Bay, 1986.

Brickhouse, Thomas C., and Nicholas D. Smith. *Plato and the Trial of Socrates.* London: Routledge, 2004.

Brown, Wendy. "*The Most We Can Hope For. . .* : Human Rights and the Politics of Fatalism." *The South Atlantic Quarterly* 103, no. 2/3 (Spring/Summer 2004): 451–463.

Bruun-Solbakk, Dávvet, and Elisabeth Stubberud. "Sápmi Pride and Queer Sápmi Organization." University of Oslo Centre for Gender Research, June 23, 2020. https://www.stk.uio.no /english/research/PRIDE/sapmi-pride.html (accessed June 1, 2021).

Burke, Edmund. *Reflections on the Revolution in France.* Oxford: Oxford University Press, 2009 [1790].

Cohen-Almagor, Raphael. "J. S. Mill's Boundaries of Freedom of Expression." *Philosophy* 92, no. 4 (2017): 565–596.

Cole, Wade M. "The Effects of Human Rights on Economic Growth, 1965 to 2010." *Sociology of Development* 2, no. 4 (2016): 375–412.

Confucius. *The Analects*. Translated by Annping Chin. London: Penguin, 2014.

Coogan, Michael D., ed. *New Oxford Annotated Bible*. 4th ed. Oxford: Oxford University Press, 2010.

Cooper, George. "Chinese State Censorship of COVID-19 Research Represents a Looming Crisis for Academic Publishers." *LSE Impact Blog*, Apr. 24, 2020. https://blogs.lse.ac.uk/impactof socialsciences/2020/04/24/chinese-state-censorship-of-covid-19-research-represents-a-looming -crisis-for-academic-publishers/ (accessed June 1, 2021).

Cranston, Maurice. *What Are Human Rights?* New York: Taplington, 1973.

Crawford, James R. *The Creation of States in International Law*. 2nd ed. Oxford: Oxford University Press, 2007.

Dalton, Russell J., Doh Chull Shin, and Willy Jou. "Popular Conceptions of the Meaning of Democracy: Democratic Understanding in Unlikely Places." UC Irvine CSD Working Papers, Center for the Study of Democracy, 2007. https://escholarship.org/uc/item/2j74b860 (accessed June 1, 2021).

Davies, Norman. *Europe: A History*. Rev. ed. Oxford: Oxford University Press, 1997.

de Bary, Wm. Theodore, and Tu Weiming, eds. *Confucianism and Human Rights*. New York: Columbia University Press, 1999.

Delgado, Richard, and Jean Stefancic. *Must We Defend Nazis?: Hate Speech, Pornography, and the New First Amendment*. New York: New York University Press, 1999.

Delgado, Richard, and Jean Stefancic. *Understanding Words That Wound*. Boulder, CO: Westview, 2004.

Denardis, Laura. *The Internet in Everything: Freedom and Security in a World with No Off Switch*. New Haven: Yale University Press, 2020.

Denham, Hannah. "These Are the Platforms That Have Banned Trump and His Allies." *Washington Post*, Jan. 12, 2021. https://www.washingtonpost.com/technology/2021/01/11/trump -banned-social-media/ (accessed June 1, 2021).

Desai, Prakash N. "Duties and Rights in Hinduism: Before and After India's Independence." In *Religious Perspectives on Bioethics and Human Rights*, edited by Joseph Tham, Kai Man Kwan, and Alberto Garcia, 155–165. Berlin: Springer, 2017.

Descartes, René. *Discours de la méthode*. In *Oeuvres et lettres*, 121–179. Paris: Gallimard [Pléiade], 1937 [1637].

Descartes, René. *Méditations*. In *Oeuvres et lettres*, 253–334. Paris: Gallimard [Pléiade], 1937 [1641].

Descartes, René. *Les passions de l'âme*. In *Oeuvres et lettres*, 691–802. Paris: Gallimard [Pléiade], 1937 [1649].

de Schutter, Olivier. *International Human Rights Law*. Cambridge: Cambridge University Press, 2014.

Dikötter, Frank. *Mao's Great Famine: The History of China's Most Devastating Catastrophe, 1958–62*. London: Bloomsbury, 2010.

Dolot, Miron. *Execution by Hunger: The Hidden Holocaust*. New York: Norton, 1987.

Donnelly, Jack. "In Search of the Unicorn: The Jurisprudence and Politics of the Right to Development." *California Western International Law Journal* 15 (1985): 473–509.

Donnelly, Jack, and Daniel Whelan. *International Human Rights*. 6th ed. New York: Routledge, 2020.

Douglas, Davison. *Jim Crow Moves North*. New York: Cambridge University Press, 2005.

Douglass, Frederick. "What to the Slave Is the Fourth of July?" (1852). *TeachingAmericanHistory.org*. https://teachingamericanhistory.org/library/document/what-to-the-slave-is-the-fourth-of-july/ (accessed June 1, 2021).

Douzinas, Costas. *The End of Human Rights Paperback*. Oxford: Hart, 2000.

Douzinas, Costas. *Human Rights and Empire: The Political Philosophy of Cosmopolitanism*. London: Routledge, 2007.

Dunn, John. *The Political Thought of John Locke: An Historical Account of the Argument of the "Two Treatises of Government."* Cambridge: Cambridge University Press, 1982.

Dworkin, Ronald. "Foreword." In *Extreme Speech and Democracy*, v–ix. Oxford: Oxford University Press, 2009.

Economist Intelligence Unit. *Democracy Index* (annual). http://www.eiu.com/ (accessed June 1, 2021).

Edney, Matthew H. *Cartography: The Ideal and Its History*. Chicago: University of Chicago Press, 2019.

Ekeli, Kristian Skagen. "Democratic Legitimacy, Political Speech and Viewpoint Neutrality." *Philosophy & Social Criticism* 47 (2021): 723–752.

Ekeli, Kristian Skagen. "Toleration, Respect for Persons, and the Free Speech Right to Do Moral Wrong." In *The Palgrave Handbook of Toleration*, edited by Mitja Sardoč, 1–24. London: Palgrave Macmillan, 2022.

Emon, Anver, Mark Ellis, and Benjamin Glahn. "From 'Common Ground' to 'Clearing Ground': A Model for Engagement in the 21st Century." In *Islamic Law and International Human Rights Law*, edited by Anver Emon, Mark Ellis, and Benjamin Glahn, 1–13. Oxford: Oxford University Press, 2012.

Erasmus, Desiderius. *The Education of a Christian Prince*. Translated by Neil M. Cheshire and Michael J. Heath, edited by Lisa Jardine. Cambridge, UK: Cambridge University Press, 1997.

Fassbender, Bardo, and Anne Peters. *The Oxford Handbook of the History of International Law*. Oxford: Oxford University Press, 2012.

Feinberg, Joel. "The Nature and Value of Rights." *Journal of Value Inquiry* 4 (1970): 143–158.

Feygin, Yakov. "Chernobyl Shows How the Soviets Squashed Scientists." *Foreign Policy*, July 11, 2019. https://foreignpolicy.com/2019/07/11/chernobyl-shows-how-the-soviets-squashed-scientists/ (accessed June 1, 2021).

Fine, Gail. "Inquiry in the *Meno*." In *The Cambridge Companion to Plato*, edited by Richard Kraut, 200–226. Cambridge, UK: Cambridge University Press, 1992.

Finnis, John. *Natural Law and Natural Rights*. 2nd ed. Oxford: Oxford University Press, 1980.

Fisher, William W. III, Morton J. Horwitz, and Thomas A. Reed, eds. *American Legal Realism*. New York: Oxford University Press, 1993.

Foner, Eric. *The Second Founding: How the Civil War and Reconstruction Remade the Constitution*. New York: Norton, 2019.

Foucault, Michel. *Le gouvernement de soi et des autres: Tome 2, Le courage de la vérité—Cours au Collège de France* 1983–1984 (Paris: Seuil, 2009).

Franck, Thomas M. "The Emerging Right to Democratic Governance." *American Journal of International Law* 86, no. 1 (1992): 46–91.

Freedman, Rosa. *The United Nations Human Rights Council: A Critique and Early Assessment*. London: Routledge, 2013.

Freedom House. https://freedomhouse.org/ (accessed June 1, 2021).

Fronza, Emanuela. *Memory and Punishment: Historical Denialism, Free Speech, and the Limits of Criminal Law*. The Hague: Asser Press, 2018.

Fuller, Lon. "Positivism and Fidelity to Law—A Reply to Professor Hart." *Harvard Law Review* 71, no. 4 (1958): 630–672.

Gadamer, Hans-Georg. *Wahrheit und Methode: Grundzüge einer philosophischen Hermeneutik*. 4th ed. Tübingen: Mohr-Siebeck, 1986.

Gaeta, Paola. *The UN Genocide Convention: A Commentary*. Oxford: Oxford University Press, 2009.

Gao, Ruiquan, and Xin Yan. "The Source of the Idea of Equality in Confucian Thought." *Frontiers of Philosophy in China* 5, no. 4 (2010): 486–505.

Gardiner, Richard. *Treaty Interpretation*. 2nd ed. Oxford: Oxford University Press, 2017.

Gilabert, Pablo. "The Importance of Linkage Arguments for the Theory and Practice of Human Rights: A Response to James Nickel." *Human Rights Quarterly* 32, no. 2 (2009–2010): 425–438.

Glendon, Mary Anne. *A World Made New*. New York: Random House, 2001.

Goyard-Fabre, Simone. *Les fondements de l'ordre juridique*. Paris: Presses Universitaires de France, 1992.

Griffin, James. *On Human Rights*. Oxford: Oxford University Press, 2008.

Guenancia, Pierre. *Descartes et l'ordre politique: Critique cartésienne des fondements de la politique*. Paris: Gallimard, 2012.

Habermas, Jürgen. *Strukturwandel der Öffentlichkeit: Untersuchungen zu einer Kategorie der bürgerlichen Gesellschaft*. Frankfurt a.M.: Suhrkamp, 1990 [1962].

Habermas, Jürgen. *Theorie des kommunikativen Handelns*. 8th ed., vol. 2. Frankfurt a.M.: Suhrkamp, 1981.

Hannum, Hurst. Review of *The Twilight of Human Rights Law*, by Eric Posner. *Human Rights Quarterly* 37 (2015): 1105–1108.

Hare, Ivan, and Weinstein, James, eds. *Extreme Speech and Democracy*. Oxford: Oxford University Press, 2009.

Hart, H. L. A. "Positivism and the Separation of Law and Morals." *Harvard Law Review* 71, no. 4 (1958): 593–629.

Hegel, Georg Wilhelm Friedrich. *Grundlinien der Philosophie des Rechts*. In *Hegel: Werke*, vol. 7. Frankfurt a.M.: Suhrkamp, 1970.

Hegel, Georg Wilhelm Friedrich. *Phänomenologie des Geistes*. In *Georg Wilhelm Friedrich Hegel: Werke*, vol. 3. Frankfurt a.M.: Suhrkamp, 1970.

Heidegger, Martin. *Über den Humanismus*. 10th ed. Frankfurt a.M.: Klostermann, 2000 [1949].

Heidegger, Martin. "Die Zeit des Weltbildes." In *Holzwege*, 10th ed. Frankfurt a.M.: Klostermann, 2015 [1950].

Heinze, Eric. "The Constitution of the Constitution: Democratic Legitimacy and Public Discourse." In *Rancière and Law*, edited by Mónica López Lerma and Julien Extabe, 111–128. New York: Routledge, 2017.

Heinze, Eric. "Democracy, Ontology, and the Limits of Deconstruction." In *Hate, Politics and Law: Critical Perspectives on Combating Hate*, edited by Thomas Brudholm and Birgitte Johanssen, 94–112. Oxford: Oxford University Press, 2018.

Heinze, Eric. "Even-handedness and the Politics of Human Rights." *Harvard Human Rights Journal* 21 (2008): 7–46.

Heinze, Eric. "Global Libertarianism: How Much Public Morality Does International Human Rights Law Allow?" *International Theory* (forthcoming, 2022).

Heinze, Eric. *Hate Speech and Democratic Citizenship*. Oxford: Oxford University Press, 2016.

Heinze, Eric. "Karl Marx's Theory of Free Speech." *Humanity Journal* (Parts 1 and 2), May 31–June 1, 2018. http://humanityjournal.org/blog/karl-marxs-theory-of-free-speech-part-1/ and http://humanityjournal.org/blog/karl-marxs-theory-of-free-speech-part-2/ (accessed June 1, 2021).

Heinze, Eric. "The Myth of Flexible Universality: Human Rights and the Limits of Comparative Naturalism." *Oxford Journal of Legal Studies* 39, no. 3 (2019): 624–653.

Heinze, Eric. Review of *La question des peuples autochtones*, by I. Schulte-Tenckhoff. *Netherlands Journal of International Law* 46 (1999): 269–276.

Heinze, Eric. *Sexual Orientation: A Human Right*. Dordrecht: Nijhoff, 1995.

Heinze, Eric. "Sexual Orientation and International Law: A Study in the Manufacture of Cross-Cultural "Sensitivity."" *Michigan Journal of International Law* 22 (2001): 283–309.

Heinze, Eric. "Taking Legitimacy Seriously: A Return to Deontology." *Constitutional Commentary* 32, no. 3 (2017): 527–583.

Heinze, Eric. "Victimless Crimes." In *Encyclopaedia of Applied Ethics*, 2nd ed., vol. 4, edited by Ruth Chadwick, 471–482. Cambridge, MA: Elsevier, 2012.

Heinze, Eric. "Viewpoint Absolutism and Hate Speech." *Modern Law Review* 69 (2006): 543–582.

Heller, Hermann. *Sovereignty: A Contribution to the Theory of Public and International Law*, edited by David Dyzenhaus. Oxford: Oxford University Press, 2019 [1927].

Henkin, Louis. *The Age of Rights*. New York: Columbia University Press, 1990.

Heyman, Steven J. "Hate Speech, Public Discourse, and the First Amendment." In *Extreme Speech and Democracy*, edited by Ivan Hare and James Weinstein, 158–181. Oxford: Oxford University Press, 2009.

Higginbotham, F. Michael. *Ghosts of Jim Crow: Ending Racism in Post-Racial America*. New York: NYU Press, 1998.

Hitler, Adolph. *Mein Kampf.* Munich: Franz Eher Verlag, 1925.

Hobbes, Thomas. *Leviathan*, edited by Christopher Brooke. Oxford: Oxford University Press, 2017.

Hobbes, Thomas. "Tomae Hobbes Malmesburiensis: Vita Carmine Expressa, Authore Seipso." In *Thomae Hobbes Malmesburiensis Opera Philosophica quae Latine Scripsit Omnia*, vol. 1, edited by William Molesworth, lxxxv–xci. London: 1839.

Hohfeld, Wesley. "Some Fundamental Legal Conceptions as Applied in Judicial Reasoning." *Yale Law Journal* 23 (1913): 16–59.

Homiak, Marcia. "Feminism and Aristotle's Rational Ideal." In *Feminism and History of Philosophy*, edited by G. Lloyd, 80–102. Oxford: Oxford University Press 1993.

Homolka, Walter, and Arnulf Heidegger, eds. *Heidegger und der Antisemitismus: Positionen im Widerstreit*. Freiburg i.B.: Herder Verlag, 2016.

Hopgood, Stephen. *The Endtimes of Human Rights Paperback*. Ithaca: Cornell University Press, 2015.

Hsi, Chu, and Lü Tsu-Ch'ien. *Reflections on Things at Hand [Chin-ssu lu]*. Translated by Wingtisit Chan. New York: Columbia University Press, 1967 [12th century CE].

Human Rights Watch. https://www.hrw.org/ (accessed June 1, 2021).

Human Rights Watch. "Russia: Government vs. Rights Groups." June 18, 2018. https://www.hrw.org/russia-government-against-rights-groups-battle-chronicle#:~:text=An%20enduring%2C%20central%20feature%20has,traitor.%E2%80%9D%20To%20date%2C%20Russia's (accessed June 1, 2021).

Hutton, Guy, Laurence Haller, and Jamie Bartram. "Global Cost-Benefit Analysis of Water Supply and Sanitation Interventions." *Journal of Water Health* 5, no. 4 (2007): 481–502.

Index on Censorship. https://www.indexoncensorship.org/ (accessed June 1, 2021).

Irvin-Erickson, Douglas. *Raphael Lemkin and the Concept of Genocide*. Philadelphia: University of Pennsylvania Press, 2016.

Jensen, Steven. *The Making of International Human Rights*. Cambridge: Cambridge University Press, 2017.

Jones, Martha S. "The US Suffragette Movement Tried to Leave out Black Women." *Guardian*, July 7, 2020. https://www.theguardian.com/us-news/2020/jul/07/us-suffragette-movement-black -women-19th-amendment (accessed June 1, 2021).

Kant, Immanuel. *Grundlegung zur Metaphysik der Sitten*. In *Werkausgabe*, vol. 7, 5–102. Frankfurt a.M.: Suhrkamp, 1968 [1785].

Kant, Immanuel. *Kritik der praktischen Vernunft*. In *Werkausgabe*, vol. 7, 104–305. Frankfurt a.M.: Suhrkamp, 1968 [1788].

Kant, Immanuel. *Die Metaphysik der Sitten*. In *Werkausgabe*, vol. 8, 303–634. Frankfurt a.M.: Suhrkamp, 1968 [1797].

Kant, Immanuel. *Über den Gemeinspruch: Das mag in der Theorie richtig sein, taugt aber nicht für die Praxis*. In *Werkausgabe*, vol. 11, 125–172. Frankfurt a.M.: Suhrkamp, 1968 [1793].

Kant, Immanuel. *Zum ewigen Frieden*. In *Werkausgabe*, vol. 8, 191–251. Frankfurt a.M.: Suhrkamp, 1968 [1795].

Kaye, David. *Speech Police: The Global Struggle to Govern the Internet*. New York: Columbia Global Reports, 2019.

Kelsen, Hans. *Reine Rechtslehre*. 2nd ed. Vienna: Mohr Siebeck, 1960.

Kelsen, Hans. *Vom Wesen und Wert der Demokratie*. Tübingen: J.C.B. Mohr, 1920.

Kennedy, David. *A World of Struggle: How Power, Law, and Expertise Shape Global Political Economy*. Princeton: Princeton University Press, 2016.

Kens, Paul. "The History and Implications of *Lochner v. New York*." Review originally published online on H-Law (2013) of David E. Bernstein's *Rehabilitating Lochner: Defending Individual Rights against Progressive Reform*. Chicago: University of Chicago Press, 2013. http://www.h-net .org/reviews/showrev.php?id=36949 (accessed June 1, 2021).

Kens, Paul. *Lochner v. New York: Economic Regulation on Trial*. Lawrence: University Press of Kansas, 1998).

Kim, Sungmoon. "Confucianism, Moral Equality, and Human Rights: A Mencian Perspective." *American Journal of Economics and Sociology* 74, no. 1 (2015): 149–185.

Kinzelbach, Katrin. "Will China's Rise Lead to a New Normative Order?: An Analysis of China's Statements on Human Rights at the United Nations." *Netherlands Quarterly of Human Rights* 30, no. 3 (2012): 299–332.

Klarman, Michael J. *From Jim Crow to Civil Rights: The Supreme Court and the Struggle for Racial Equality*. New York: Oxford University Press, 2006.

Kolesnik-Antoine, Delphine. *Descartes: La politique des passions*. Paris: Presses Universitaires de France, 2011.

Koob, Sigrid Alexandra, Stinne Skriver Jørgensen, and Hans-Otto Sano. "Human Rights and Economic Growth: An Econometric Analysis of Freedom and Participation Rights." Danish Institute for Human Rights, 2017. https://www.humanrights.dk/publications/human-rights -economic-growth (accessed June 1, 2021).

Koskenniemi, Martti. *From Apology to Utopia: The Structure of International Legal Argument*. Cambridge: Cambridge University Press, 2006.

Kühnhardt, Ludger. *Die Universalität der Menschenrechte*. Munich: Olzog, 1987.

Langlois, Anthony J. "Human Rights without Democracy—A Critique of the Separationist Thesis." *Human Rights Quarterly* 25 (2003): 990–1019.

Langton, Rae. "Speech Acts and Unspeakable Acts." *Philosophy and Public Affairs* 22 (1993): 305–330.

Lauterpacht, Hersch. *An International Bill of the Rights of Man*. Cambridge, UK: Cambridge University Press, 2013.

Leggewie, Claus and Horst Meier. 2002. *Verbot der NPD oder mit Rechtsradikalen leben?* Frankfurt a.M.: Suhrkamp.

Leiter, Brian. *Naturalizing Jurisprudence: Essays on American Legal Realism and Naturalism in Legal Philosophy*. New York: Oxford University Press, 2007.

Lloyd, S. A., ed. *The Bloomsbury Companion to Hobbes*. London: Bloomsbury, 2013.

Locke, John. *Second Treatise of Government* and *A Letter Concerning Toleration*. Oxford: Oxford University Press, 2016.

Loy, David. "A Different 'Enlightened' Jurisprudence?." *Saint Louis University Law Journal* 54 (2010): 1239–1256.

Manent, Pierre. *La loi naturelle et les droits de l'homme*. Paris: Presses Universitaires de France, 2018.

Marks, Susan. "Human Rights and Root Causes." *Modern Law Review* 74 (2011): 57–78.

Martel, James R. *Subverting the Leviathan: Reading Thomas Hobbes as a Radical Democrat*. New York: Columbia University Press, 2007.

Martinich, A. P. *The Two Gods of Leviathan: Thomas Hobbes on Religion and Politics*. New York: Cambridge University Press, 1992.

Martinich, A. P., and Kinch Hoekstra, eds. *The Oxford Handbook of Hobbes*. Oxford: Oxford University Press, 2016.

Marx, K. "Kritik des Gothaer Programms." In *Karl Marx—Friedrich Engels: Werke*, vol. 19, edited by IML/ZK-SED, 11–34. Berlin: Dietz, 1956+ [1875].

Marx, K. "Zur Judenfrage." In *Karl Marx—Friedrich Engels: Werke*, 6th ed., vol. 1, edited by IML/ZK-SED, 347–377. Berlin: Dietz, 1956+ [1844].

Marx, K. "Zur Kritik der Hegelschen Rechtsphilosophie." In *Karl Marx—Friedrich Engels: Werke*, vol. 1, edited by IML/ZK-SED [Institut für Marxismus-Leninismus beim Zentralkomitee der SED], 201–333. Berlin: Dietz, 1956+ [1844].

Matsuda, Mary, Charles Lawrence III, Richard Delgado, and Kimberlé Crenshaw, eds. *Words That Wound: Critical Race Theory, Assaultive Speech, and the First Amendment*. Boulder, CO: Westview Press. 1993.

McGinnis, John O., and Ilya Somin. "Democracy and International Human Rights Law." *Notre Dame Law Review* 84, no. 4 (2009): 1739–1798.

McGrogan, David. *Critical Theory and Human Rights: From Compassion to Coercion*. Manchester, UK: Manchester University Press, 2021.

Memmi, Albert. *Portrait du colonisé/Portrait du colonisateur*. Paris: Gallimard, 2002.

Menke, Christoph. *Kritik der Rechte*. Frankfurt a.M.: Suhrkamp, 2015.

Menke, Christoph, and Arnd Pollmann. *Philosophie der Menschenrechte*. 4th ed. Hamburg: Junius, 2017.

Merleau-Ponty, Maurice. *Phénoménologie de la perception*. Paris: Gallimard, 1945.

Mill, John Stuart. *On Liberty and Other Essays*, edited by John Gray. Oxford: Oxford University Press, 1991 [1869].

"Ministry of Finance of Kyrgyzstan Will Compensate for Death in Prison." ACCA Media, Dec. 7, 2019. https://acca.media/en/ministry-of-finance-of-kyrgyzstan-will-compensate-for-death-in -prison/ (accessed June 1, 2021).

Minow, Martha. "Interpreting Rights: An Essay for Robert Cover." *Yale Law Journal* 96, no. 8 (July 1987): 1860–1915.

Minow, Martha. "Rights for the Next Generation: A Feminist Approach to Children's Rights." *Harvard Women's Law Journal* 9, no. 1 (1986): 1–24.

Morsink, Johannes. *The Universal Declaration of Human Rights: Origins, Drafting, and Intent*. Philadelphia: University of Pennsylvania Press, 2000.

Moyn, Samuel. *Christian Human Rights*. Philadelphia: University of Pennsylvania Press, 2017.

Moyn, Samuel. *The Last Utopia: Human Rights in History*. Cambridge, MA: Harvard University Press, 2010.

Mutua, Makau. 2008. *Human Rights: A Political and Cultural Critique*. Philadelphia: University of Pennsylvania Press.

Nedelsky, Jennifer. *Relations of Freedom and Law's Relations*. Cambridge University Press, 2012.

Nehring, Andreas. "Human Rights in the Context of Buddhism." In *Human Rights and Religion in Educational Contexts*, edited by Manfred L. Pirner, Johannes Lähnemann, and Heiner Bielefeldt, 127–136. Berlin: Springer, 2016.

Nickel, James W. "Indivisibility and Linkage Arguments: A Reply to Gilabert." *Human Rights Quarterly* 32, no. 2 (2009–2010): 439–446.

Nickel, James W. *Making Sense of Human Rights*. 2nd ed. Malden: Blackwell, 2007.

Nickel, James W. "Rethinking Indivisibility: Towards a Theory of Supporting Relations between Human Rights." *Human Rights Quarterly* 30, no. 4 (2008): 984–1001.

Nowak, John, and Ronald Rotunda. *Constitutional Law*. 8th ed. St. Paul, MN: West Academic Publishing, 2009.

Nuovo, Victor. Review of *God, Locke and Equality*, by Jeremy Waldron. *Notre Dame Philosophical Reviews*, May 4, 2003. https://ndpr.nd.edu/news/god-locke-and-equality-christian-foundations -of-locke-s-political-thought/ (accessed July 1, 2020).

Nuyen, A. T. "Confucianism and the Idea of Equality." *Asian Philosophy* 11, no. 2 (2010): 61–71.

O'Byrne, Darren J. "Marxism and Human Rights: New Thoughts on an Old Debate." *The International Journal of Human Rights* 23, no. 4 (2019): 638–652.

Olechowski, Thomas. *Hans Kelsen: Biographie eines Rechtswissenschaftlers*. Vienna: Mohr Siebeck, 2020.

Orakhelashvili, Alexander. *Akehurst's Modern Introduction to International Law*. London: Routledge, 2018.

Orakhelashvili, Alexander. *Peremptory Norms in International Law*. Oxford: Oxford University Press, 2006.

Padilla, E. "Intergenerational Equity and Sustainability." *Ecological Economics* 41 (2002): 69–83.

Palmer, David A. "Daoism and Human Rights: Integrating the Incommensurable." In *Religious Perspectives on Bioethics and Human Rights*, edited by Joseph Tham, Kai Man Kwan, and Alberto Garcia, 139–144. Berlin: Springer, 2017.

Pedersen, Ole W. "The European Court of Human Rights and International Environmental Law." In *The Human Right to a Healthy Environment*, edited by John H. Knox and Ramin Pejan, 86–96. Cambridge, UK: Cambridge University Press, 2018.

Plato. *Plato: Complete Works*, edited by J. M. Cooper. Indianapolis: Hackett, 1997.

Popper, Karl. *The Open Society and Its Enemies*. Vols. 1–2. London: Routledge 1995 [1945].

Posner, Eric. *The Twilight of Human Rights Law*. Oxford: Oxford University Press, 2014.

Post, Robert. *Constitutional Domains: Democracy, Community, Management*. Cambridge, MA: Harvard University Press, 1995.

Post, Robert. "Hate Speech." In *Extreme Speech and Democracy*, edited by Ivan Hare and James Weinstein, 123–138. Oxford: Oxford University Press, 2009.

Post, Robert. "Participatory Democracy and Free Speech." *Virginia Law Review* 97, no. 3 (2011): 477–490.

Prott, Volker. *The Politics of Self-Determination: Remaking Territories and National Identities in Europe 1917–1923.* Oxford: Oxford University Press, 2016.

"Putin Denounces Opponents Who Receive Foreign Money." *Expatica*, Dec. 12, 2012. https://www.expatica.com/ru/uncategorized/putin-denounces-opponents-who-receive-foreign-money-74895/ (accessed June 1, 2021).

Quintavalla, Alberto, and Klaus Heine. "Priorities and Human Rights." *International Journal of Human Rights* 23, no. 4 (2018): 679–697.

Qur'an. Translated by M. A. Abdel Haleem. London: Oxford University Press, 2004.

Rawls, John. *The Law of Peoples.* Cambridge, MA: Harvard University Press, 1999.

Rémy, Vanessa, Nathalie Largeron, Sibilia Quilici, and Stuart Carroll. "The Economic Value of Vaccination: Why Prevention Is Wealth." *Journal of Market Access and Health Policy*, Aug. 12, 2015. https://www.ncbi.nlm.nih.gov/pmc/articles/PMC4802701/ (accessed June 1, 2021).

Rehman, Javaid. *International Human Rights Law.* 2nd ed. Harlow, UK: Longman 2010.

Reporters Without Borders. *World Press Freedom Index* (annual). https://rsf.org/en/ranking (accessed June 1, 2021).

Rhodes, Aaron. *The Debasement of Human Rights: How Politics Sabotage the Ideal of Freedom.* New York: Encounter, 2018.

Rousseau, Jean-Jacques. *Du Contrat Social.* In *Oeuvres Complètes*, vol. 3, 347–470. Paris: Gallimard [Pléiade], 1964.

Rousseau, Jean-Jacques. *Émile* I. In *Oeuvres Complètes*, vol. 4, 239–868. Paris: Gallimard [Pléiade], 1969.

Saeed, Abdullah. *Human Rights and Islam: An Introduction to Key Debates between Islamic Law and International Human Rights Law.* Cheltenham, UK: Elgar, 2018.

Sang-Jin, Han. "Confucianism and Human Rights." In *Confucianism in Context: Classic Philosophy and Contemporary Issues, East Asia and Beyond*, edited by Wonsuk Chang and Leah Kalmanson, 89–99. New York: SUNY Press, 2010.

San José, Daniel García. *Environmental Protection and the European Convention on Human Rights.* Strasbourg: Council of Europe, 2005.

Sartre, Jean-Paul. *L'Être et le Néant: Essai d'ontologie phénoménologique.* Paris: Gallimard, 1943.

Sartre, Jean-Paul. *L'Existentialisme est un humanisme.* Paris: Gallimard 1996 [1945].

Schauer, Frederick. "Formalism." *Yale Law Journal* 97 (1988): 509–548.

Schmidt-Leukel, Perry. "Buddhism and the Idea of Human Rights: Resonances and Dissonances." *Buddhist-Christian Studies* 26 (2006): 33–49.

Schmitt, Carl, *Der Leviathan in der Staatslehre des Thomas Hobbes*. Stuttgart: Klett-Cotta, 1982 [1938].

Schrijver, Nico. "Fifty Years International Human Rights Covenants: Improving the Global Protection of Human Rights by Bridging the Gap between the Two Covenants." *NTM-NJCM Bulletin* no. 33 (2016) 457–464.

Sen, Amartya. "Freedom Favors Development." *New Perspectives Quarterly* 3, no. 4 (1996): 23–27.

Shah, Shantichandra B. "Human Rights—From Jain Perspective." *Revue Québécoise de droit international* 11, no. 2 (1998): 263–266.

Shakespeare, William. *Henry VI, Part Two*, edited by Roger Warren. Oxford: Oxford University Press, 2003.

Sharma, Arvind. *Hinduism and Human Rights: A Conceptual Approach*. Oxford: Oxford University Press, 2004.

Shelton, Dinah. Review of *The Twilight of International Law*, by Eric Posner. *American Journal of International Law* 109, no. 1 (2015): 228–234.

Sikkink, Kathryn. *Evidence for Hope: Making Human Rights Work in the 21st Century*. Princeton: Princeton University Press, 2020.

Sim, Cameron. "The Singapore Chill: Political Defamation and the Normalization of a Statist Rule of Law." *Pacific Rim Law & Policy Journal* 20, no. 2 (2011): 319–353.

Sim, May. "A Confucian Approach to Human Rights." *History of Philosophy Quarterly* 21, no. 4 (2004): 337–356.

Social Progress Imperative. *Social Progress Index* (annual). https://www.socialprogress.org/ (accessed Apr. 1, 2021).

Sorell, Tom, ed. *The Cambridge Companion to Hobbes*. Cambridge, UK: Cambridge University Press, 1996.

Steiner, Henry J. "Political Participation as a Human Right." *Harvard Human Rights Yearbook* 1 (1988): 77–134.

Stewart, Nikita. "'We Are Committing Educational Malpractice': Why Slavery Is Mistaught—and Worse—in American Schools." *New York Times*, Aug. 19, 2021. https://www.nytimes.com /interactive/2019/08/19/magazine/slavery-american-schools.html (accessed June 1, 2021).

Stolzenberg, Nomi, and Gideon Yaffe. "Waldron's Locke and Locke's Waldron: Review of Jeremy Waldron's *God, Locke and Equality*." *Inquiry* 49, no. 2 (2006): 186–216.

Strauss, Leo. "Hobbes' politische Wissenschaft und zugehörige Schriften." In *Gesammelte Schriften*, vol. 3. Berlin: Luchterhand, 1965.

Strossen, Nadine. *HATE: Why We Should Resist It with Free Speech, Not Censorship*. Oxford: Oxford University Press, 2012.

Tarasco, Martha. "Hinduism and Human Rights." In *Religious Perspectives on Bioethics and Human Rights*, edited by Joseph Tham, Kai Man Kwan, and Alberto Garcia, 173–180. Berlin: Springer, 2017.

Thiel, Markus, ed. *Wehrhafte Demokratie: Beiträge über die Regelungen zum Schutze der freiheitlichen demokratischen Grundordnung.* Tübingen: Mohr Siebeck, 2003.

Tierney, Brian. *The Idea of Natural Rights.* Atlanta: Emory University Press, 1997.

Tiwald, Justin. "Confucianism and Human Rights." In *Routledge Handbook of Human Rights*, edited by Thomas Cushman, 244–254. London: Routledge, 2011.

Tönnies, Ferdinand. *Gemeinschaft und Gesellschaft: Grundbegriffe der reinen Soziologie.* Munich: Profil, 2016.

Tourkochoriti, Ioanna. *Freedom of Expression: An Inquiry into The Revolutionary Roots of American and French Legal Thought.* Cambridge, UK: Cambridge University Press, 2021.

Transparency International. *Corruption Perceptions Index* (annual). https://www.transparency .org/en/cpi (accessed June 1, 2021).

"'Transphobe' Julie Bindel Banned from Free Speech Debate." *The Mancunion*, Oct. 6, 2015. https://mancunion.com/2015/10/06/transphobe-julie-bindel-banned-from-free-speech-debate/ (accessed Jan. 4, 2021) (unsigned article).

Trawny, Peter. *Heidegger und der Mythos der jüdischen Weltverschwörung.* 3rd ed. Frankfurt a.M.: Klostermann, 2015.

Uzgalis, William. "John Locke, Racism, Slavery, and Indian Lands." In *The Oxford Handbook of Philosophy and Race*, edited by Naomi Zack, 21–31. Oxford: Oxford University Press, 2017.

Vanderlinden, Jacques. *Anthropologie juridique.* Paris: Dalloz 1996.

Viansson-Ponté, Pierre. "Quand la France s'ennuie." *Le Monde*, Mar. 15, 1968.

Vlastos, Gregory. *Platonic Studies.* 2nd ed. Princeton: Princeton University Press, 1981.

Waldron, Jeremy. "The Conditions of Legitimacy." *Constitutional Commentary* 32 (2017): 697–714.

Waldron, Jeremy. *God, Locke and Equality: Christian Foundations of Locke's Political Thought.* Cambridge, UK: Cambridge University Press, 2002.

Waldron, Jeremy. *The Harm in Hate Speech.* Boston: Harvard University Press, 2012.

Waldron, Jeremy. "Hate Speech and Political Legitimacy." In *The Content and Context of Hate Speech: Rethinking Regulation and Responses*, edited by Michael Herz and Peter Molnar, 329–340. Cambridge: Cambridge University Press, 2012.

Waldron, Jeremy. "Hobbes and the Principle of Publicity." *Pacific Philosophical Quarterly* 82 (2001): 447–474.

Walker, S. Jay. "Frederick Douglass and Woman Suffrage." *The Black Scholar* 4, no. 6/7 (1973): 24–31.

Ward, Ian, and Clare Mcglyn. "Would John Stuart Mill Have Regulated Pornography?," *Journal of Law and Society* 41, no. 4 (2014): 500–522.

Warren, Samuel, and Louis Brandeis. "The Right to Privacy." *Harvard Law Review* 4, no. 5 (1890): 193–220.

Weinstein, James. "Hate Speech Bans, Democracy, and Political Legitimacy." *Constitutional Commentary* 32, no. 3 (2017): 527–583.

Weinstein, James. "Hate Speech Bans and Political Legitimacy: A Reply." *Constitutional Commentary* 32, no. 3 (2017): 715–782.

Weinstein, James. "An Overview of American Free Speech Doctrine and Its Application to Extreme Speech." In *Extreme Speech and Democracy*, edited by Ivan Hare and James Weinstein, 81–95. Oxford: Oxford University Press, 2009.

"Wesley Newcomb Hohfeld." Unsigned obituary. *Yale Law Journal* 28 (1918): 166–168.

Whelan, Daniel J. *Indivisible Human Rights: A History*. Philadelphia: University of Pennsylvania Press, 2010.

Wittgenstein, Ludwig. *Philosophische Untersuchungen*. In *Werkausgabe*, vol. 1, 225–580. Frankfurt a.M.: Suhrkamp, 1984 [1953]).

Wolton, Thierry. *Le Négationnisme de gauche*. Paris: Grasset, 2019.

Index

Dictators, 2, 31–33, 40, 54, 59, 73, 75, 78–79, 105

Differentialism
adaptation and, 16–20
ambiguity and, 16–20
Christianity and, 13
civic, 11
concept of human rights and, 11–22, 24, 141n1, 142n10
Confucianism and, 13
discrimination and, 145n1
egalitarianism and, 12–22, 24, 43–44, 141n1, 142n10
formalism and, 20–24
individualism and, 15, 43–44
managerialism and, 11, 19
realism and, 20–24
Universal Declaration of Human Rights and, 15

Dignity, 4, 41, 68, 118, 133–134, 139

Discourse on Method (Descartes), 34

Discrimination
Convention on the Elimination of All Forms of Discrimination against Women (CEDAW) and, 59, 63
differentialism and, 141n1
duty principle and, 52
free speech and, 117–119, 121, 123
International Convention on the Elimination of All Forms of Racial Discrimination (ICERD) and, 59, 63, 117–118
ITP Convention and, 26
racial, 59, 63, 86, 117–118, 126
sex, 5
Universal Declaration of Human Rights and, 3, 73, 121, 135, 139
women and, 3, 59, 144n5

Discursive principle
Bradwell v. Illinois and, 80, 82
conflict and, 79
Dred Scott v. Sandford and, 80, 82

duty principle and, 60, 80, 82, 89, 100, 151n12
free speech and, 79–84, 89, 92, 95, 100, 118–119, 151n12, 152nn15–17
Hohfeld and, 83
Kelsen and, 83
legal issues and, 60, 79–84, 89, 92, 95, 100, 118–119, 151n12, 152nn15–17
Plessy v. Ferguson and, 80, 82
Universal Declaration of Human Rights and, 81, 89, 100

Dix, Otto, 40

Döblin, Alfred, 40

Doctors for Life, 114–115

Donnelly, Jack, 83–84

Douglas, William O., 111–112, 115

Douglass, Frederick, 49, 60, 89, 127

Dred Scott v. Sandford, 43, 45, 51, 80, 82

Drugs, 55, 64, 85

Dunn, John, 146n47

Duty principle
discrimination and, 52
discursive principle and, 60, 80, 82, 89, 100, 151n12
free speech and, 80, 82, 89, 100
global context and, 52–55, 60, 70
Hohfeld and, 52, 55, 60, 70, 127
Kelsen and, 55, 60, 70, 127
legal issues and, 52–55, 60, 70, 80, 82, 89, 100, 127–128, 151n12
Universal Declaration of Human Rights and, 54

Economist (journal), 93

Egalitarianism
adaptation and, 16–20
ambiguity and, 16–20
capitalism and, 37, 45, 123
civic, 12, 24
concept of human rights and, 11–24, 125, 145n1, 142n10

Freedom (cont.)

concept of human rights and, 2, 5, 11, 15, 22, 141n2

of contract, 44

costs of rights and, 64–67

from fear and want, 133

greatest possible, 102

individualism and, 25–26, 28, 34, 44, 65, 150n32

opinions and, 101–102, 104–106, 110, 115, 118–119, 121, 124

religious, 5, 15, 58, 65, 68, 73, 85, 104, 115, 140

of thought, 59

Universal Declaration of Human Rights and, 133–134, 138, 140–141

Freedom Day, 2

Free expression, 84, 88, 100, 102, 152nn15, 17, 153n18

Free speech

absolutism and, 101–106, 109–110, 114, 117–124

abuse and, 86, 94, 98, 105, 109, 114–115

activists and, 74, 88, 95, 123

belief systems and, 81, 100

Bindel and, 122–123

blasphemy and, 103, 109–110

Brandenburg v. Ohio and, 116–118

censorship and, 95, 103–104, 112–113, 115, 120–121, 129, 149n13, 153n26

Cohen v. California and, 112–114

concept of human rights and, 5–9, 11, 15–16, 125, 129, 141n1, 151n12, 152nn15–16, 153nn24, 26

conflict and, 79, 117, 122, 126

consent and, 91–92, 108

content and, 102–107

democracy and, 9, 84–94, 101, 106, 116, 118, 121, 129, 153nn24, 26

discrimination and, 117–119, 121, 123

discursive principle and, 79–84, 89, 92, 95, 100, 118–119, 151n12, 152nn15–17

Doctors for Life and, 114–115

duty principle and, 80, 82, 89, 100

Enlightenment and, 90, 120

ethics and, 92, 103–104

extreme speech and, 103, 109, 116–124, 129, 157n58

Feiner v. New York and, 110–115

fighting words and, 107–110, 113, 117, 120, 124, 129

flag burning and, 155n9

free expression and, 84, 88, 100, 102, 152nn15, 17, 153n18

global context and, 55, 60–62, 65–66

harm principle and, 102–103

hate speech and, 103, 117–119, 151n12, 153n24

health and, 78, 80, 86, 98, 123

human goods and, 74, 81–82, 86–88, 96–98, 100, 104, 122

international law and, 63, 75, 84–85, 91–92, 112

justice and, 81, 85–86, 89, 99, 106, 110–116

Ku Klux Klan and, 116

legal issues and, 73, 76–79, 83–87, 90, 94, 100–102, 104, 109, 116–117, 151n9

liberty and, 102–103

managerialism and, 8, 11, 74, 76, 81–82, 89, 92, 95–100, 121, 128

moral issues and, 89, 91, 116

opinions and, 101–124, 158n1, 155n25

pornographic, 103

public expression and, 80, 129, 151n12

public forum and, 109–115, 155n25

public sphere and, 7–8, 11, 15, 74, 81–82, 94, 101, 104, 107–115, 117, 120–123, 129–130, 141n1, 151n12, 152n15

racism and, 101, 103, 109, 117

Reporters Without Borders and, 101, 149n13, 154n1

rights as claims and, 75–79

slavery and, 114